Cooking for the Family

Cooking
for the Family

Rosemary Wadey

OCTOPUS

Contents

First published in 1981 by
Octopus Books Limited
59 Grosvenor Street
London W1

This edition published in 1983

ISBN 0 7064 2010 1

Printed in Hong Kong

Introduction

Each day women everywhere are faced with the task of feeding their families. It sounds simple enough but after a while it can become tedious attempting to think of new ideas and trying to budget wisely.

As children grow older they tend to become more demanding, appearing at odd times and creating havoc with set meal times. Children's tastes change too: they move from baby food to simple fare and finally to the same as everyone else. With their appetites seemingly increasing daily, there are times when they can eagerly consume more than anyone else in the family. Therefore the cook in the family has to cater for the children's changing needs – and their food fads – as well as satisfy the grown-up members of the family, who usually object to 'nursery food', or fish fingers and beans. Another consideration is that whatever is presented to the family must also supply a good balance of vitamins and nutrients.

A housewife and mother has so many demands on her time that complicated preparation and cooking methods are out. Instead she must look for short cuts and those recipes which require little attention during cooking, combined with reasonably priced ingredients. However, in all families there are occasions when something special is required and a little experimentation can be instilled into the daily planning in order to create a grander dish.

The recipes in this book have been chosen to give ideas for all sorts of occasions from quick teatime snacks to more elaborate dishes and menus.

A little forethought in both planning and shopping can save a great deal of time and energy. For large family gatherings many of the recipes, such as the casseroles, roasts and pies may be doubled up; or made in larger quantities so there is sufficient left over to eat the next day, or to be cooled rapidly and frozen.

Cooking for a family need not be a daily chore; it can be an interesting and enjoyable challenge, particularly for the cook who is prepared to experiment. On busy days it can be turned into an easy task which requires the very minimum of attention. Whatever the circumstances this book gives some interesting new ideas and a range of recipes that will encourage and please both the cook and her family.

High Teas and Suppers

After school, after work, before or after a visit to the theatre or cinema, anything from a modest snack to a fairly substantial meal may be wanted. A dish which can be prepared, or at least partly prepared, in advance is a help, and the cooking should be neither too long nor complicated. Quiches or flans, spaghetti and pasta dishes, soups and chowders all fit the bill. Recipes which are especially quick and easy to make are denoted by a Q symbol followed by the number of minutes it takes to prepare and cook them.

Red bean chowder

Metric	Imperial
100 g red kidney beans, soaked in water overnight, or 1 × 425 g can red kidney beans and 300 ml beef stock	*4 oz red kidney beans, soaked in water overnight, or 1 × 15 oz can red kidney beans and ½ pint beef stock*
175 g finely minced beef	*6 oz finely minced beef*
1 large onion, peeled and finely chopped	*1 large onion, peeled and finely chopped*
1 × 425 g can tomatoes	*1 × 15 oz can tomatoes*
1 × 5 ml spoon tomato purée	*1 teaspoon tomato purée*
450 ml beef stock	*¾ pint beef stock*
salt	*salt*
freshly ground black pepper	*freshly ground black pepper*
about 1 × 5 ml spoon chilli powder	*about 1 teaspoon chilli powder*
1 × 5 ml spoon cornflour	*1 teaspoon cornflour*

Preparation time: 10–15 minutes, plus soaking time
Cooking time: about 1¼ hours, plus cooking the dried beans, if used

Chilli powder is very hot and varies in strength according to the brand used, so use it cautiously.

If using dried beans, drain and place in a saucepan with enough water to cover. Bring to the boil, then boil for 10 minutes. Cover and simmer for 1½ hours. Drain and reserve 300 ml/½ pint of the cooking liquid. Cook the mince in a pan over a gentle heat with no extra fat for 5 minutes, stirring occasionally. Add the onion and continue cooking for a further 5 minutes. Add the tomatoes, tomato purée, stock, salt and pepper, chilli powder and the drained beans with the reserved liquid. If using canned beans drain and rinse under cold running water, and add with the extra beef stock. Bring to the boil, cover and simmer gently for about 1 hour.
Take off the heat, taste and adjust the seasoning, add the cornflour blended in a little cold water and bring back to the boil. Serve in bowls with hot crusty bread.

Quick mushroom and tomato pizza

Metric	Imperial
150 g self-raising flour	*6 oz self-raising flour*
salt	*salt*
freshly ground black pepper	*freshly ground black pepper*
40 g butter or margarine	*1½ oz butter or margarine*
40 g Cheddar cheese, grated	*1½ oz Cheddar cheese, grated*
1 small onion, peeled and grated	*1 small onion, peeled and grated*
1 egg	*1 egg*
1–2 × 15 ml spoons milk	*1–2 tablespoons milk*

Topping:	**Topping**
100 g pork boiling ring, skinned and thinly sliced	*4 oz pork boiling ring, skinned and thinly sliced*
4 tomatoes, skinned and sliced or 1 × 425 g can tomatoes, drained	*4 tomatoes, skinned and sliced or 1 × 15 oz can tomatoes, drained*
25 g butter or margarine	*1 oz butter or margarine*
100 g mushrooms, sliced	*4 oz mushrooms, sliced*
1 × 2.5 ml spoon dried basil or oregano	*½ teaspoon dried basil or oregano*
75 g Cheddar cheese, grated	*3 oz Cheddar cheese, grated*

Preparation time: 10 minutes
Cooking time: 30 minutes
Oven: 220°C, 425°F, Gas Mark 7

To make the pizza base, sift the flour into a bowl with the salt and pepper and rub in the fat until the mixture resembles fine breadcrumbs. Mix in the cheese and onion, then add the egg and sufficient milk to mix to a fairly soft dough. On a floured surface roll out the dough to a circle about 22 cm/8½ inches in diameter and place on a greased baking sheet.
Lay the slices of pork boiling ring over the dough then cover with the sliced or drained tomatoes. Melt the butter and gently fry the mushrooms for 1–2 minutes, then spoon these over the tomatoes. Sprinkle with the herbs, salt and pepper and then with the cheese. Bake in a preheated oven for 25–30 minutes until the scone base is well risen and the topping golden brown. Serve hot.

Red bean chowder, Quick mushroom and tomato pizza

Fish chowder

Metric	Imperial
25 g butter or margarine	1 oz butter or margarine
1 onion, peeled and finely chopped	1 onion, peeled and finely chopped
225 g smoked haddock or smoked cod fillet, (fresh or frozen), roughly chopped	8 oz smoked haddock or smoked cod fillet, (fresh or frozen), roughly chopped
450 ml water	¾ pint water
450 ml milk	¾ pint milk
freshly ground black pepper	freshly ground black pepper
1 bay leaf	1 bay leaf
75–100 g long-grain rice	3–4 oz long-grain rice
dash of Worcestershire sauce	dash of Worcestershire sauce
1 × 15 ml spoon lemon juice	1 tablespoon lemon juice
pinch of ground nutmeg	pinch of ground nutmeg
salt	salt
2 × 15 ml spoons chopped fresh parsley	2 tablespoons chopped fresh parsley
1 hard-boiled egg, finely grated, to garnish	1 hard-boiled egg, finely grated, to garnish

Preparation time: 5 minutes
Cooking time: about 30 minutes

Melt the butter or margarine in a pan, add the onion and fry gently until soft and lightly browned. Stir in the fish and mix thoroughly, then add the water and milk and bring to the boil. Season well with pepper only (smoked fish tends to be very salty) and add the bay leaf, rice, Worcestershire sauce, lemon juice and nutmeg. Cover and simmer gently for about 25 minutes or until the rice is tender and the fish well broken up, stirring occasionally.
Adjust the seasoning, stir in the parsley and serve very hot, topping each portion with a spoonful of grated hard-boiled egg. Serve with crisp rolls and butter.

Fish chowder, Curried soup, Leek and potato soup

Curried soup

Metric	Imperial
40 g margarine	1½ oz margarine
1 onion, peeled and finely chopped	1 onion, peeled and finely chopped
100 g carrots, peeled and coarsely grated	4 oz carrots, peeled and coarsely grated
1 × 15 ml spoon plain flour	1 tablespoon plain flour
2–3 × 5 ml spoons curry powder	2–3 teaspoons curry powder
1 × 5 ml spoon tomato purée	1 teaspoon tomato purée
900 ml chicken stock	1½ pints chicken stock
salt	salt
freshly ground black pepper	freshly ground black pepper
25 g long-grain rice	1 oz long-grain rice
4 × 15 ml spoons finely chopped cooked meat or poultry (optional)	4 tablespoons finely chopped cooked meat or poultry (optional)
about 300 ml milk or stock	about ½ pint milk or stock

Preparation time: 5 minutes
Cooking time: 45 minutes

Melt the margarine in a saucepan and gently fry the onion and grated carrots until soft and the onion is only just beginning to colour. Stir in the flour, curry powder, tomato purée, stock, salt and pepper, and bring to the boil. Add the rice, cover and simmer for 30 minutes or until the contents are very tender. Add the meat or poultry, and sufficient milk or stock to give the required consistency. Simmer for a further 5 minutes, taste and adjust the seasoning and serve.

Leek and potato soup

Metric
40 g margarine
2 large leeks, trimmed
    and sliced
350 g potatoes, peeled
    and roughly chopped
450–600 ml chicken stock
pinch of ground mace
salt
freshly ground black
    pepper
300 ml milk
croûtons, to garnish

Imperial
1½ oz margarine
2 large leeks, trimmed
    and sliced
12 oz potatoes, peeled
    and roughly chopped
¾–1 pint chicken stock
pinch of ground mace
salt
freshly ground black
    pepper
½ pint milk
croûtons, to garnish

Preparation time: 10 minutes
Cooking time: about 30 minutes

Melt the margarine in a saucepan and gently fry the leeks until soft. Add the potatoes, stock, mace, salt and pepper and bring to the boil. Cover and simmer gently for about 20 minutes, or until very tender.
Cool slightly then blend or sieve the mixture and return it to a clean pan. Add the milk, bring to the boil and adjust the seasoning. (Extra milk may be added for a thinner soup.) Serve with bread croûtons.

Variation:
In place of the leeks 2 large onions may be used and the soup garnished with crisply-fried chopped bacon.

Chicken macaroni bake

Preparation time: 15 minutes
Cooking time: about 1 hour
Oven: 200°C, 400°F, Gas Mark 6

Metric
225 g macaroni
salt
50 g butter or margarine
1 large onion, peeled and
    sliced
40 g plain flour
450 ml milk or chicken
    stock
1 × 5 ml spoon dried
    mixed herbs
225 g cooked chicken or
    turkey meat, chopped
freshly ground black
    pepper
75 g Cheddar cheese,
    grated
1 × 200 g can tomatoes or
    3 tomatoes, skinned
    and sliced
parsley sprigs, to garnish

Imperial
8 oz macaroni
salt
2 oz butter or margarine
1 large onion, peeled and
    sliced
1½ oz plain flour
¾ pint milk or chicken
    stock
1 teaspoon dried mixed
    herbs
8 oz cooked chicken or
    turkey meat, chopped
freshly ground black
    pepper
3 oz Cheddar cheese,
    grated
1 × 7 oz can tomatoes or
    3 tomatoes, skinned
    and sliced
parsley sprigs, to garnish

Cook the macaroni in plenty of boiling salted water until just tender. Drain thoroughly, rinse under hot running water and drain again. Meanwhile melt the butter and fry the onion until light golden brown. Stir in the flour and cook for 1 minute. Gradually add the milk or stock and bring to the boil for 2 minutes. Stir in the herbs, chopped meat, salt, pepper and half of the grated cheese.

Place two-thirds of the macaroni in a greased casserole, pour on the sauce, then cover with the remaining macaroni. Lay the tomatoes over the macaroni, sprinkle with the remaining cheese and bake in a pre-heated oven for about 40 minutes, until bubbling hot and the top is golden brown. Garnish with the parsley. Serve with a crunchy mixed salad or coleslaw.

Variation:
This is a marvellous way to use leftover meats. Boiled bacon could be used instead of chicken.

Spaghetti with ham and tomato sauce

Metric	Imperial
2 × 15 ml spoons oil	2 tablespoons oil
1 onion, peeled and chopped	1 onion, peeled and chopped
1 red pepper, seeded and chopped	1 red pepper, seeded and chopped
225 g tomatoes, skinned and sliced	8 oz tomatoes, skinned and sliced
150 ml stock	¼ pint stock
1 × 15 ml spoon tomato purée	1 tablespoon tomato purée
1 × 5 ml spoon dry mustard	1 teaspoon dry mustard
salt	salt
freshly ground black pepper	freshly ground black pepper
100 g mushrooms, sliced	4 oz mushrooms, sliced
225 g cooked ham or bacon, chopped or minced	8 oz cooked ham or bacon, chopped or minced
225 g spaghetti	8 oz spaghetti
1 × 15 ml spoon grated Parmesan cheese	1 tablespoon grated Parmesan cheese
chopped fresh parsley, to garnish	chopped fresh parsley, to garnish
grated Parmesan cheese, to serve	grated Parmesan cheese, to serve

Preparation time: 15–20 minutes
Cooking time: 25–30 minutes

Heat the oil in a pan and gently fry the onion and pepper until tender. Add the tomatoes, stock, tomato purée, mustard, salt and pepper, and bring to the boil. Simmer uncovered, for about 10 minutes, stirring occasionally, until tender. Stir in the mushrooms and chopped ham or bacon, adjust the seasoning and cook for 3–4 minutes.

Meanwhile cook the spaghetti in a large saucepan of boiling salted water for about 12 minutes or until just tender – do not overcook.

Drain the spaghetti, rinse under hot running water and drain again. Mix in the cheese and place on a heated serving dish. Spoon the sauce on top, sprinkle with parsley and serve with extra Parmesan cheese.

Spaghetti with ham and tomato sauce,
Chicken macaroni bake, Fish lasagne

Fish lasagne

Metric	Imperial
350 g cod fillet, skinned	12 oz cod fillet, skinned
about 600 ml milk	about 1 pint milk
salt	salt
freshly ground black pepper	freshly ground black pepper
1 × 15 ml spoon oil	1 tablespoon oil
8 sheets green lasagne (about 175 g)	8 sheets green lasagne (about 6 oz)
75 g butter or margarine	3 oz butter or margarine
1 onion, peeled and chopped	1 onion, peeled and chopped
100 g mushrooms, chopped	4 oz mushrooms, chopped
1 red pepper, seeded and chopped or 2 caps canned red pepper, drained and chopped	1 red pepper, seeded and chopped or 2 caps canned red pepper, drained and chopped
1 × 200 g can tuna fish, drained and flaked	1 × 7 oz can tuna fish, drained and flaked
50 g plain flour	2 oz plain flour
50 g Cheddar cheese, grated	2 oz Cheddar cheese, grated

Preparation time: 25 minutes
Cooking time: 1 hour
Oven: 200°C, 400°F, Gas Mark 6

Place the cod in a pan, pour on only enough milk to cover, and add salt and pepper. Bring to the boil, cover and simmer gently for 8–10 minutes until tender. Leave to cool.

Bring a large pan of salted water to the boil and add the oil. Cook the lasagne, four sheets at a time for about 11 minutes until just tender. Drain and place on a clean cloth to dry.

Melt 25 g/1 oz of the butter in a pan and fry the onion until soft. Add the mushrooms and pepper and continue frying for 2–3 minutes, then take off the heat. Drain the cod and make the liquid up to 600 ml/1 pint with the remaining milk, and set on one side. Flake the cod, removing any remaining bones, and mix with the tuna fish.

Melt the remaining butter in a pan, stir in the flour and cook for 1 minute. Gradually add the milk stirring continuously, bring to the boil – and cook for 2 minutes. Add salt and pepper then stir three-quarters of the sauce into the mushroom mixture.

Place two sheets of lasagne in a greased shallow casserole to cover the bottom. Cover with one-third of the fish and one-third of the mushroom mixture. In this way continue layering the rest of the lasagne, fish and mushroom mixture finishing with a layer of lasagne. Pour the remaining white sauce over the lasagne and sprinkle with grated cheese. Cook in a preheated oven for about 40 minutes or until well browned and bubbling.

13

Pork and liver terrine

Metric
225 g belly pork, rind removed
225 g pig's liver
1 onion, peeled
175 g streaky bacon rashers, rind removed
1–2 garlic cloves, peeled and crushed
freshly ground black pepper
large pinch of ground allspice
1 egg, beaten
2 × 15 ml spoons sherry or brandy

To garnish:
tomatoes
cucumber slices

Imperial
8 oz belly pork, rind removed
8 oz pig's liver
1 onion, peeled
6 oz streaky bacon rashers, rind removed
1–2 garlic cloves, peeled and crushed
freshly ground black pepper
large pinch of ground allspice
1 egg, beaten
2 tablespoons sherry or brandy

To garnish:
tomatoes
cucumber slices

Preparation time: 10 minutes
Cooking time: 1¼ hours
Oven: 180°C, 350°F, Gas Mark 4

Finely mince the pork, liver, onion and 2 rashers of the bacon. Add the garlic, plenty of salt and pepper, the allspice, beaten egg, sherry or brandy and mix together thoroughly.
Stretch the remaining bacon rashers with the back of a knife and use to line the inside of a greased 450 g/ 1 lb loaf tin. Spoon in the mixture and fold over the ends of the bacon. Place this in a roasting tin containing 4 cm/1½ inches water and cook in a preheated oven for 1¼ hours. Allow to cool slightly then cover with a weighted plate to keep the top flat and leave until cold. Cover tightly and chill.
Garnish with tomato and cucumber slices and serve with buttered toast, crusty bread, or oatcakes.

Pizza baps

Metric
4 brown or white baps
175 g streaky bacon rashers, rind removed, chopped
1 large onion, peeled and thinly sliced
salt
freshly ground black pepper
4–5 tomatoes, sliced
100–175 g Mozzarella or Gouda cheese, thinly sliced
1 × 50 g can anchovies, drained
16 stuffed green or stoned black olives (optional)
watercress, to garnish

Imperial
4 brown or white baps
6 oz streaky bacon rashers, rind removed, chopped
1 large onion, peeled and thinly sliced
salt
freshly ground black pepper
4–5 tomatoes, sliced
4–6 oz Mozzarella or Gouda cheese, thinly sliced
1 × 2 oz can anchovies, drained
16 stuffed green or stoned black olives (optional)
watercress, to garnish

Preparation time: 10 minutes
Cooking time: about 5 minutes

Split the baps in half and toast each piece lightly on both sides. Place in a grill pan, cut sides upwards. Fry the bacon gently in a frying pan until the fat runs, then add the onion and continue frying gently until the bacon and onion are cooked and lightly browned. Season with salt and pepper and divide between the baps, spreading evenly over each one. Cover with slices of tomato and then a slice or two of the cheese. Make a cross design on each bap half with pieces of anchovy fillet and place sliced olives in the corners. Cook under a preheated moderate grill for 3–5 minutes or until the cheese is bubbling and brown. Serve hot, garnished with watercress.

Sardine and cheese pâté

Preparation time: 5 minutes

Metric
1 × 200 g can sardines in
  oil, drained
75 g packet full fat soft
  cheese
2 hard-boiled eggs
1 × 5 ml spoon lemon juice
salt
freshly ground black
  pepper
1 garlic clove, peeled and
  crushed or a pinch of
  garlic powder
1 × 15 ml spoon cream or
  plain unsweetened
  yogurt
40 g butter, melted
sliced cucumber, to
  garnish

Imperial
1 × 7 oz can sardines in
  oil, drained
3 oz packet full fat soft
  cheese
2 hard-boiled eggs
1 teaspoon lemon juice
salt
freshly ground black
  pepper
1 garlic clove, peeled and
  crushed or a pinch of
  garlic powder
1 tablespoon cream or
  plain unsweetened
  yogurt
1½ oz butter, melted
sliced cucumber, to
  garnish

Mash the sardines and beat in the soft cheese evenly. Finely grate the hard-boiled eggs into the mixture, adding the lemon juice, salt, pepper and garlic. Mix thoroughly and beat in the cream or yogurt. Taste and adjust the seasoning and spoon into one serving dish or four individual dishes. Cover with a thin layer of melted butter and chill until set.
Garnish the pâté with slices of cucumber and serve with rolls, French bread or toast, and a salad.

Pizza baps, Sardine and cheese pâté, Pork and liver terrine

Curried eggs

Metric	Imperial
40 g margarine	1½ oz margarine
1 × 15 ml spoon oil	1 tablespoon oil
2 onions, peeled and finely chopped	2 onions, peeled and finely chopped
1 garlic clove, peeled and crushed	1 garlic clove, peeled and crushed
1 × 15 ml spoon curry powder	1 tablespoon curry powder
1½ × 15 ml spoons plain flour	1½ tablespoons plain flour
2 × 5 ml spoons tomato purée	2 teaspoons tomato purée
pinch each of ground ginger, ground cloves and ground cinnamon	pinch each of ground ginger, ground cloves and ground cinnamon
450 ml chicken stock	¾ pint chicken stock
2 × 15 ml spoons sweet pickle or chutney	2 tablespoons sweet pickle or chutney
40 g sultanas	1½ oz sultanas
1 eating apple, peeled, cored and chopped	1 eating apple, peeled, cored and chopped
salt	salt
freshly ground black pepper	freshly ground black pepper
225 g long-grain rice	8 oz long-grain rice
8 eggs	8 eggs

Preparation time: 10 minutes
Cooking time: 50 minutes

Serve this dish with individual side dishes of a sliced tomato and onion salad, sliced bananas dipped in lemon juice, chopped green pepper and salted peanuts. Bought poppadums are a good accompaniment.

Heat the margarine and oil in a pan and gently fry the onions and garlic until soft and lightly coloured. Stir in the curry powder, flour, tomato purée, ginger, cloves and cinnamon and cook for 2 minutes. Gradually add the stock, stirring, and bring to the boil. Stir in the pickle, sultanas, apple, salt and pepper. Cover and simmer for about 40 minutes, stirring occasionally. Adjust the seasoning to taste.
Meanwhile, cook the rice in boiling salted water until just tender, then drain thoroughly. Hard-boil the eggs for 10 minutes (or poach if preferred) place them in a warm dish surrounded by the rice and pour over the curry sauce.

Variation:
This curry sauce makes a good base for other types of curry, simply add 225–350 g/8–12 oz of any diced cooked meat or flaked fish towards the end and heat through for several minutes. Serve on a bed of rice and accompanied by the side dishes.

Chicken and almond rissoles

Metric	Imperial
225 g mashed potato	8 oz mashed potato
2 × 15 ml spoons minced or finely chopped onion, or finely chopped spring onions or chives	2 tablespoons minced or finely chopped onion, or finely chopped spring onions or chives
175 g cooked chicken, minced	6 oz cooked chicken, minced
salt	salt
freshly ground black pepper	freshly ground black pepper
garlic powder (optional)	garlic powder (optional)
pinch of ground mace	pinch of ground mace
1 egg, beaten	1 egg, beaten
about 50 g blanched almonds, finely chopped	about 2 oz blanched almonds, finely chopped
fat for frying	fat for frying

To garnish:	To garnish:
tomato slices	tomato slices
mustard and cress	mustard and cress

Preparation time: 10 minutes
Cooking time: about 10 minutes

Combine the mashed potato, onion and minced chicken and season well with salt, pepper, garlic powder and mace. Add about one-third of the beaten egg and mix thoroughly. Divide into 8 portions and shape into sausage shapes or flat round cakes. Dip in or brush with the remaining beaten egg and coat in the chopped almonds.
Fry the rissoles gently in shallow fat for about 4 minutes on each side or until golden brown and piping hot. Drain on kitchen paper and serve hot, garnished with sliced tomatoes and mustard and cress. Italian Tomato Sauce (page 18) or Mustard Sauce (page 51) can be served with these rissoles.

Variation:
Cooked turkey meat or any other cooked meat may be used in place of cooked chicken. Instant mashed potato may also be used.

Chicken and almond rissoles, Curried eggs

Omelettes with Italian tomato sauce

25

Metric	Imperial
25 g butter	1 oz butter
1 small onion, peeled and finely chopped	1 small onion, peeled and finely chopped
1 garlic clove, peeled and crushed	1 garlic clove, peeled and crushed
1 × 200 g can tomatoes	1 × 7 oz can tomatoes
150 ml stock	¼ pint stock
1 × 15 ml spoon tomato purée	1 tablespoon tomato purée
1 × 2.5–5 ml spoon dried basil	½–1 teaspoon dried basil
generous dash of Worcestershire sauce	generous dash of Worcestershire sauce
1 × 2.5 ml spoon sugar	½ teaspoon sugar
salt	salt
freshly ground black pepper	freshly ground black pepper

Omelettes:	Omelettes:
8 eggs	8 eggs
4 × 15 ml spoons water	4 tablespoons water
dried basil (optional)	dried basil (optional)
50 g butter	2 oz butter
parsley sprigs, to garnish	parsley sprigs, to garnish

Preparation time: 15 minutes
Cooking time: about 10 minutes

This sauce is also good served with grilled or fried meats and fish.

First make the tomato sauce. Melt the butter in a pan, add the onion and garlic and fry gently until soft and lightly coloured. Sieve or purée the tomatoes in a blender, and add to the pan with the stock, tomato purée, basil, Worcestershire sauce, sugar and salt and pepper. Bring to the boil and simmer, uncovered, for about 5 minutes or until thickened and smooth.
Meanwhile, make the omelettes. Each omelette requires 2 eggs, 1 × 15 ml spoon/1 tablespoon water, a generous pinch of basil, and salt and pepper to taste, all beaten together. Melt 15 g/½ oz of the butter in an omelette or small frying pan and when hot pour in enough egg mixture for one omelette. Cook gently, continuously pulling the setting egg to the centre of pan with a fork and allowing the liquid egg to run out to the sides of the pan. When just set all over, fold carefully into three and slide on to a warm plate. Keep warm while making the remaining 3 omelettes.
Serve the omelettes with the sauce poured over, garnished with parsley, and accompanied by crisp French bread.

Cauliflower cheese soufflé

Metric	Imperial
1 medium cauliflower, cut into florets	1 medium cauliflower, cut into florets
salt	salt
50 g butter	2 oz butter
50 g plain flour	2 oz plain flour
300 ml milk	½ pint milk
100 g mature Cheddar cheese, grated	4 oz mature Cheddar cheese, grated
1 × 5 ml spoon made mustard	1 teaspoon made mustard
1 × 2.5 ml spoon Worcestershire sauce	½ teaspoon Worcestershire sauce
freshly ground black pepper	freshly ground black pepper
3 eggs (sizes 1, 2), separated	3 eggs (sizes 1, 2), separated
1 egg white	1 egg white

Preparation time: 15 minutes
Cooking time: about 1 hour
Oven: 190°C, 375°F, Gas Mark 5

Try to resist opening the oven door while the soufflé is rising or it will sink at once.

Cook the cauliflower in boiling salted water until tender but still crisp. Drain and place in a buttered 1.5 litre/2½ pint soufflé dish or other straight-sided oven-proof dish.
Melt the butter in a pan, stir in the flour and cook for 1 minute. Gradually add the milk over a low heat and bring to the boil, stirring continuously to give a thick smooth sauce. Simmer for 2 minutes, then remove from the heat and stir in the cheese, mustard, Worcestershire sauce, salt, pepper and egg yolks. Whisk the 4 egg whites until stiff, beat 2 × 15 ml spoons/ 2 tablespoons of the whites into the sauce, then fold in the remainder.
Pour the sauce over the cauliflower and cook the soufflé in a preheated oven for about 50 minutes, until well risen with a golden top. Serve immediately straight from the oven.

Egg and potato fritters

25

Preparation time: 10 minutes
Cooking time: 15 minutes

Metric

750 g potatoes, peeled
   and grated
1 large onion, peeled and
   grated
salt
freshly ground black
   pepper
pinch of ground nutmeg
1 egg yolk
1 × 15 ml spoon grated
   Parmesan cheese
3 × 15 ml spoons oil
4 eggs (sizes 1, 2)
75 g Cheddar cheese,
   grated

Imperial

1½ lb potatoes, peeled
   and grated
1 large onion, peeled and
   grated
salt
freshly ground black
   pepper
pinch of ground nutmeg
1 egg yolk
1 tablespoon grated
   Parmesan cheese
3 tablespoons oil
4 eggs (sizes 1, 2)
3 oz Cheddar cheese,
   grated

Mix the potatoes and onion with plenty of salt and pepper, the nutmeg, egg yolk and Parmesan cheese. Heat the oil in a large frying pan and spoon in four equal portions of the potato mixture, pressing each one flat with a palette knife. Fry each side for about 5 minutes, turning the mixture over carefully, until golden brown and cooked through. Drain on kitchen paper and keep warm on a flameproof dish.

Either fry or poach the eggs, place one on each potato fritter and sprinkle with the Cheddar cheese.

Place the fritters briefly under a preheated hot grill until the cheese just begins to melt and serve at once.

Omelettes with Italian tomato sauce, Cauliflower cheese soufflé, Egg and potato fritters

High tea toasts

Metric	*Imperial*
4 thick slices bread	*4 thick slices bread*
butter	*butter*
2 × 15 ml spoons chutney	*2 tablespoons chutney*
4 tomatoes, sliced	*4 tomatoes, sliced*
175 g Cheddar cheese,	*6 oz Cheddar cheese,*
grated	*grated*
8 streaky bacon rashers,	*8 streaky bacon rashers,*
rind removed	*rind removed*

Preparation time: 10 minutes

Toast the bread on each side, then butter each slice and spread with the chutney. Arrange the tomato slices on top, sprinkle on the cheese and return the slices to the preheated moderate grill for a few minutes until golden brown.
Meanwhile fry the bacon until crispy. Top each toast with two rashers of bacon and serve at once.

Hamburger pancakes, High tea toasts, Sardine scramble toasts

Hamburger pancakes

Metric
100 g plain flour
salt
freshly ground black
   pepper
1 egg
150 ml beef stock
150 ml milk
1 medium onion, peeled
   and grated
350 g minced beef
4 × 15 ml spoons tomato
   chutney

Imperial
4 oz plain flour
salt
freshly ground black
   pepper
1 egg
¼ pint beef stock
¼ pint milk
1 medium onion, peeled
   and grated
12 oz minced beef
4 tablespoons tomato
   chutney

Preparation time: 10 minutes
Cooking time: 10–15 minutes

Sift the flour into a bowl and add salt and pepper.
Make a well in the centre, add the egg, stock and milk,
then beat to a smooth batter. Stir in the grated onion
and the minced beef.
Lightly grease a griddle or large non-stick frying pan.
Allowing 2 × 15 ml spoons/2 tablespoons mixture per
pancake cook 4 small pancakes until set on one side.
Flip the pancakes over and cook for a further 2 to 3
minutes. Keep the cooking pancakes warm while you
cook the remaining batter, making 8 small pancakes.
Sandwich the hamburger pancakes together in pairs
with the tomato chutney.
Serve with fried onions and a tossed green salad.

Sardine scramble toasts

Metric
2 × 175 g cans sardines in
   oil, drained
grated rind and juice of
   ½ lemon
salt
freshly ground black
   pepper
2 × 15 ml spoons chopped
   fresh parsley
6 eggs
100 g butter
4 slices toast, lightly
   buttered
1 × 15 ml spoon capers

Imperial
2 × 6 oz cans sardines in
   oil, drained
grated rind and juice of
   ½ lemon
salt
freshly ground black
   pepper
2 tablespoons chopped
   fresh parsley
6 eggs
4 oz butter
4 slices toast, lightly
   buttered
1 tablespoon capers

Preparation time: 10 minutes
Cooking time: 15 minutes

Mash the sardines in a bowl with the lemon juice and
salt and pepper to taste. Stir in the chopped parsley.
Beat the eggs in a bowl with salt and pepper. Melt
25 g/1 oz of the butter in a small pan and add the
egg mixture. Stir over a gentle heat until the eggs
scramble. Spread the sardine mixture over each slice
of buttered toast, and top with the hot scrambled egg.
Heat the remaining butter in a pan with the lemon rind
and capers until bubbling, then spoon over each slice
of toast and topping, and serve. If preferred grill the
sardine mixture before adding the scrambled egg.

Cheese and vegetable flan

Metric
75 g plain flour
75 g wholemeal flour
pinch of salt
40 g margarine
40 g lard
1 × 15 ml spoon grated
    Parmesan cheese
about 2 × 15 ml spoons
    cold water

Filling:
100 g carrots, peeled and
    diced
3 sticks celery, sliced
1 leek, trimmed and sliced
salt
50 g butter
1 onion, peeled and thinly
    sliced
100 g mushrooms, sliced
25 g plain flour
250 ml milk
freshly ground black
    pepper
75 g Cheddar cheese,
    grated

Imperial
3 oz plain flour
3 oz wholemeal flour
pinch of salt
1½ oz margarine
1½ oz lard
1 tablespoon grated
    Parmesan cheese
about 2 tablespoons cold
    water

Filling:
4 oz carrots, peeled and
    diced
3 sticks celery, sliced
1 leek, trimmed and sliced
salt
2 oz butter
1 onion, peeled and thinly
    sliced
4 oz mushrooms, sliced
1 oz plain flour
8 fl oz milk
freshly ground black
    pepper
3 oz Cheddar cheese,
    grated

Preparation time: 15 minutes
Cooking time: about 30 minutes
Oven: 200°C, 400°F, Gas Mark 6

Place the flours and salt in a bowl and rub in the fats until the mixture resembles fine breadcrumbs. Mix in the Parmesan cheese, then add sufficient water to make a pliable dough. Roll out and use to line a 20 cm/8 inch flan ring or dish. Bake blind (by lining the pastry with greaseproof paper and half filling with dried beans) in a preheated oven for 15–20 minutes. Remove the paper and beans and return the pastry to the oven for about 5 minutes to let it dry out.
Meanwhile cook the carrots, celery and leek in the minimum of boiling salted water without letting it boil dry, until just tender, then drain. Melt the butter in a saucepan and fry the onion until soft. Add the mushrooms and continue frying for 2–3 minutes, stir in the flour and cook for 1 minute. Gradually add the milk, stirring, and bring to the boil. Add salt and pepper, stir in the vegetables and simmer for 3 minutes. Stir in the cheese and pour into the flan case. Serve hot. This is a good accompaniment to grilled chops.

Leek and bacon quiche

Metric
150 g plain flour
pinch of salt
40 g butter or margarine
40 g lard
about 2 × 15 ml spoons
    cold water, to mix

Filling:
25 g butter or margarine
1 medium leek (about
    225 g), thinly sliced
175 g collar bacon
    rashers, rind removed,
    chopped
50 g mature Cheddar
    cheese, grated
2 eggs
125 ml milk
125 ml single cream
salt
freshly ground black
    pepper
pinch of ground nutmeg

Imperial
6 oz plain flour
pinch of salt
1½ oz butter or margarine
1½ oz lard
about 2 tablespoons
    cold water, to mix

Filling:
1 oz butter or margarine
1 medium leek (about
    8 oz), thinly sliced
6 oz collar bacon
    rashers, rind removed,
    chopped
2 oz mature Cheddar
    cheese, grated
2 eggs
¼ pint milk
¼ pint single cream
salt
freshly ground black
    pepper
pinch of ground nutmeg

Preparation time: 15 minutes
Cooking time: about 50 minutes
Oven: 220°C, 425°F, Gas Mark 7
    180°C, 350°F, Gas Mark 4

To make the pastry, sift the flour and salt into a bowl, rub in the fats until the mixture resembles fine breadcrumbs, then add sufficient water to mix to a pliable dough. Wrap in polythene and chill.
Heat the butter or margarine in a pan and gently fry the leeks and bacon for 3–4 minutes until soft. Drain well on kitchen paper.
Roll out the pastry and use to line either a 20 cm/ 8 inch flan ring placed on a baking sheet, or a flan dish. Spoon the leek and bacon mixture over the base and sprinkle with the cheese. Beat the eggs, milk, cream, salt, pepper and nutmeg together and pour into the pastry case. Bake in a preheated oven for 20–25 minutes until lightly browned.
Reduce the oven temperature and cook for a further 15–20 minutes until golden brown and firm to the touch. Serve hot or cold.

Chicken liver pots, Cheese and vegetable flan,
Leek and bacon quiche

Chicken liver pots

Metric
225 g chicken livers
150 ml stock
salt
freshly ground black
   pepper
25 g butter
1 medium onion, peeled
   and finely chopped
1 garlic clove, peeled and
   crushed (optional)
2 hard-boiled eggs
1 × 15 ml spoon sherry
   or brandy
tomato or stuffed olives,
   to garnish

Imperial
8 oz chicken livers
¼ pint stock
salt
freshly ground black
   pepper
1 oz butter
1 medium onion, peeled
   and finely chopped
1 garlic clove, peeled and
   crushed (optional)
2 hard-boiled eggs
1 tablespoon sherry
   or brandy
tomato or stuffed olives,
   to garnish

Preparation time: 10 minutes, plus chilling time
Cooking time: 20 minutes

Trim and place the livers in a small pan with the stock, salt and pepper, bring to the boil and simmer for 10 minutes. Drain and reserve the cooking liquid.
Melt the butter in a small pan and fry the onion and garlic until lightly coloured. Mince the drained livers with the onion and hard-boiled eggs or purée in an electric blender until smooth. Stir in the sherry or brandy, 1 × 15 ml spoon/1 tablespoon of the reserved cooking liquid, and salt and pepper to taste. Divide between 4 individual dishes and chill until set.
Garnish with slices of stuffed olives or tomato and serve with hot toast or crusty rolls and butter.

Seafood quiche

Metric	Imperial
150 g plain flour	6 oz plain flour
pinch of salt	pinch of salt
40 g margarine	1½ oz margarine
40 g lard	1½ oz lard
about 2 × 15 ml spoons cold water	about 2 tablespoons cold water

Filling:	Filling:
225 g white fish fillet, poached	8 oz white fish fillet, poached
2 tomatoes, skinned and sliced	2 tomatoes, skinned and sliced
100 g peeled prawns	4 oz peeled prawns
1 × 15 ml spoon chopped fresh parsley	1 tablespoon chopped fresh parsley
2 eggs	2 eggs
200 ml milk	⅓ pint milk
salt	salt
freshly ground black pepper	freshly ground black pepper
pinch of garlic powder	pinch of garlic powder
2 × 5 ml spoons anchovy essence	2 teaspoons anchovy essence
pinch of ground nutmeg	pinch of ground nutmeg
50 g Cheddar cheese, thinly sliced or grated	2 oz Cheddar cheese, thinly sliced or grated

Preparation time: 25 minutes
Cooking time: 40–45 minutes
Oven: 220°C, 425°F, Gas Mark 7
      180°C, 350°F, Gas Mark 4

To make the pastry, sift the flour and salt into a bowl, rub in the fats until the mixture resembles fine breadcrumbs, then add sufficient water to mix to a pliable dough. Wrap in polythene or greaseproof paper and chill for at least 15 minutes.

Meanwhile flake the white fish fillet, discarding any bones and skin.

Roll out the pastry and line a 20 cm/8 inch flan ring or dish. Place the fish in the pastry case. Cover with the sliced tomatoes, then with the prawns and sprinkle with parsley. Beat together the eggs, milk, salt and pepper to taste, garlic, anchovy essence, nutmeg and pour the mixture over the fish.

Bake in a preheated oven for 20 minutes. Lay or sprinkle the cheese on top of the filling, reduce the oven temperature and cook for a further 20 minutes or until set and golden brown. Serve hot or cold.

Variation:
Canned tuna fish or poached smoked haddock may be used in place of white fish but leave out the anchovy essence.

Kipper risotto

20

Metric	Imperial
1 × 275 g packet frozen 'boil in the bag' kipper fillets	1 × 10 oz packet frozen 'boil in the bag' kipper fillets
25 g butter	1 oz butter
1 onion, peeled and thinly sliced	1 onion, peeled and thinly sliced
100 g peas, cooked	4 oz peas, cooked
2–3 × 15 ml spoons cream or top of the milk	2–3 tablespoons cream or top of the milk
2 hard-boiled eggs, chopped (optional)	2 hard-boiled eggs, chopped (optional)
salt	salt
freshly ground black pepper	freshly ground black pepper
1 × 275 g can 'Ready Cooked' rice or 225 g freshly boiled rice	1 × 10 oz can 'Ready Cooked' Rice or 8 oz freshly boiled rice

Preparation time: 5 minutes
Cooking time: 15 minutes

Cook the kipper fillets in the bag in a pan of boiling water according to the directions on the packet. Meanwhile, melt the butter in a fairly large pan, add the onion and fry until soft and lightly coloured. Stir in the peas, cream or milk, eggs, salt and pepper, and heat through gently.

Heat the 'Ready Cooked' rice, if using, as directed on the can. Stir the heated or freshly boiled rice into the onion mixture. Drain the kippers, remove from the bag and flake the fish, discarding any bones and the skin. Add to the risotto and mix well. Heat through quickly, adjust the seasoning and serve.
Serves 3

Left: Kipper risotto, Seafood quiche. Below: Tuna fish crumble

Tuna fish crumble

Metric	Imperial
1 × 15 ml spoon oil	1 tablespoon oil
1 large onion, peeled and sliced	1 large onion, peeled and sliced
1 × 300 g can condensed cream of mushroom soup	1 × 11 oz can condensed cream of mushroom soup
salt	salt
freshly ground black pepper	freshly ground black pepper
1 × 200 g can tuna fish, drained and roughly flaked	1 × 7 oz can tuna fish, drained and roughly flaked
3–4 hard-boiled eggs, sliced	3–4 hard-boiled eggs, sliced
50 g fresh breadcrumbs	2 oz fresh breadcrumbs
50 g Cheddar cheese, grated	2 oz Cheddar cheese, grated
tomato slices, to garnish	tomato slices, to garnish

Preparation time: about 15 minutes
Cooking time: 20–25 minutes
Oven: 220°C, 425°F, Gas Mark 7

Heat the oil in a saucepan, add the onion and fry until golden brown. Stir in the undiluted mushroom soup and bring to the boil. Season well with salt and pepper. Lay the tuna fish in a shallow ovenproof dish. Arrange the eggs on top and cover with the mushroom soup mixture. Combine the breadcrumbs and cheese and scatter in a thick layer over the soup. Cook in a preheated oven for about 30 minutes or until well browned. Garnish with slices of tomato.
Serves 3–4

Variations:
Condensed cream of celery or tomato soup may be used in place of mushroom.

Main Dishes

The main family meal of the day usually revolves around a substantial dish that features meat, poultry or fish. The dish must be appetizing and attractive in order to tempt all the family, and the accompanying vegetables should complement it as well as provide a well-balanced meal. The recipes here use the cheaper cuts of meat and less popular types of fish to produce nutritious – and delicious – fare that will not overstretch the budget.

Cidered beef casserole

Metric
500 g chuck steak, cubed
25 g seasoned flour
3 × 15 ml spoons oil
1 large onion, peeled and
    sliced
1 garlic clove, peeled and
    crushed
300 ml cider
150 ml beef stock
2 large carrots, peeled
    and cut into sticks
3–4 celery sticks, sliced
1 × 5 ml spoon French
    mustard
salt
freshly ground black
    pepper

Imperial
1¼ lb chuck steak, cubed
1 oz seasoned flour
3 tablespoons oil
1 large onion, peeled and
    sliced
1 garlic clove, peeled and
    crushed
½ pint cider
¼ pint beef stock
2 large carrots, peeled
    and cut into sticks
3–4 celery sticks, sliced
1 teaspoon French
    mustard
salt
freshly ground black
    pepper

Preparation time: 10–15 minutes
Cooking time: 1½ hours
Oven: 180°C, 350°F, Gas Mark 4

Toss the meat in the seasoned flour until evenly coated.
Heat 2 × 15 ml spoons/2 tablespoons of the oil in a
frying pan, add the meat and fry until browned all
over. Transfer the meat to a casserole.
Add the remaining oil, the onion and garlic to the
frying pan and fry gently until lightly coloured. Stir
in any remaining seasoned flour, then gradually stir
in the cider and stock and bring to the boil. Add the
carrots, celery and mustard and simmer for 2 minutes.
Add salt and pepper and pour into the casserole.
Cover and cook in a preheated oven for about 1½ hours
or until the meat is tender. Adjust the seasoning and
serve with boiled potatoes, or pasta, and a green
vegetable.

Variation:
Pale ale may be used in place of cider, in which case
stir in 1 × 5 ml spoon/1 teaspoon brown sugar with
the French mustard.

Minted lamb pie, Cidered beef casserole

Minted lamb pie

Metric
150 g plain flour
pinch of salt
110 g hard margarine,
    chilled
about 6 × 15 ml spoons
    cold water

Filling:
1 × 15 ml spoon dripping
450 g lean lamb, diced
1 large onion, peeled and
    sliced
3 celery sticks, sliced
300 ml stock
1½ × 5 ml spoons dried
    mint, or 1 × 15 ml spoon
    chopped fresh mint
salt
freshly ground black
    pepper
1½ × 5 ml spoon cornflour
150 ml milk
75 g cooked peas
    (optional)
beaten egg, to glaze

Imperial
6 oz plain flour
pinch of salt
4½ oz hard margarine,
    chilled
about 6 tablespoons
    cold water

Filling:
1 tablespoon dripping
1 lb lean lamb, diced
1 large onion, peeled and
    sliced
3 celery sticks, sliced
½ pint stock
1½ teaspoons dried
    mint, or 1 tablespoon
    chopped fresh mint
salt
freshly ground black
    pepper
1½ teaspoons cornflour
¼ pint milk
3 oz cooked peas
    (optional)
beaten egg, to glaze

Preparation time: 20–25 minutes
Cooking time: 1 hour
Oven: 220°C, 425°F, Gas Mark 7

To make the rough puff pastry, sift the flour and salt
into a bowl. Coarsely grate the margarine into the
flour and mix well. Add sufficient water to mix to a
firm dough. Roll out the dough to a narrow strip. Fold
the bottom third up and the top third down. Seal the
edges by pressing with a rolling pin and give the
dough a quarter turn so the folds are at the side.
Repeat the rolling out and folding twice more, then
wrap in polythene and chill while making the filling.
Melt the dripping in a pan, add the lamb and fry
quickly to seal on all sides. Add the onion and celery
and cook gently for 10 minutes. Stir in the stock, mint,
salt and pepper and bring to the boil. Cover and
simmer for 20 minutes, until the lamb is tender.
Dissolve the cornflour in the milk. Add to the pan with
the peas and simmer for 2 minutes. Pour into a pie
dish and leave to cool for about 20 minutes.
Roll out the dough on a floured surface. Cut out a strip
wide enough to place round the dampened rim of the
dish. Brush this strip with water, then place the lid
on top. Trim the edges, flake with a knife and crimp.
Make a hole in the centre and decorate with leaves
made from dough trimmings. Brush with beaten egg
and bake in a preheated oven for 30–40 minutes or
until well risen, and golden brown. Serve hot.

Meatballs with spicy tomato sauce

Metric	Imperial
450 g minced lamb or beef	1 lb minced lamb or beef
½ onion, peeled and grated	½ onion, peeled and grated
2 × 15 ml spoons Military or sweet pickle	2 tablespoons Military or sweet pickle
salt	salt
freshly ground black pepper	freshly ground black pepper
1 egg yolk	1 egg yolk
flour for coating	flour for coating
40 g butter or margarine	1½ oz butter or margarine

Sauce:

Metric	Imperial
1 large onion, peeled	1 large onion, peeled
1 × 425 g can tomatoes	1 × 15 oz can tomatoes
1 × 15 ml spoon plain flour	1 tablespoon plain flour
1 × 15 ml spoon tomato purée	1 tablespoon tomato purée
3 × 15 ml spoons Military or sweet pickle	3 tablespoons Military or sweet pickle
1 × 5 ml spoon Worcestershire sauce	1 teaspoon Worcestershire sauce
150 ml stock	¼ pint stock
salt	salt
freshly ground black pepper	freshly ground black pepper
chopped fresh parsley, to garnish	chopped fresh parsley, to garnish

Preparation time: 10 minutes
Cooking time: 1 hour
Oven: 180°C, 350°F, Gas Mark 4

Combine the beef, grated onion, pickle and salt and pepper to taste and bind with the egg yolk. Divide into 20 equal portions and shape each into a ball. Coat lightly in flour.

Melt the butter or margarine in a frying pan. Add the meatballs, in batches, and brown on all sides. As the meatballs are browned, transfer them to a casserole with a slotted spoon.

To make the sauce, chop the onion and purée with the tomatoes in an electric blender, or finely chop both the onion and tomatoes. Pour off all but 1 × 15 ml spoon/1 tablespoon of the fat from the frying pan, stir in the flour and cook for 1 minute. Add the tomato mixture, the tomato purée, pickle, Worcestershire sauce, stock and salt and pepper to taste. Bring to the boil, stirring, and simmer for 2–3 minutes, then pour over the meatballs.

Cover and cook in a preheated oven for about 45 minutes. Garnish with parsley and serve with pasta.

Minced beef and potato pie

Metric	Imperial
450 g minced beef	1 lb minced beef
1 onion, peeled and thinly sliced	1 onion, peeled and thinly sliced
1 × 15 ml spoon plain flour	1 tablespoon plain flour
grated rind of ½ orange	grated rind of ½ orange
juice of 1 orange	juice of 1 orange
1 × 200 g can tomatoes	1 × 7 oz can tomatoes
4 × 15 ml spoons beef stock	4 tablespoons beef stock
1 × 2.5 ml spoon Worcestershire sauce	½ teaspoon Worcestershire sauce
salt	salt
freshly ground black pepper	freshly ground black pepper
75 g Cheddar cheese, grated	3 oz Cheddar cheese, grated
750 g potatoes, peeled, cooked and mashed	1½ lb potatoes, peeled, cooked and mashed
fresh parsley, to garnish	fresh parsley, to garnish

Preparation time: 10 minutes
Cooking time: about 1 hour
Oven: 200°C, 400°F, Gas Mark 6

Cook the meat gently in a pan without any extra fat for 4–5 minutes or until browned. Add the onion and continue cooking for 5 minutes. Stir in the flour followed by the orange rind and juice, tomatoes, stock, Worcestershire sauce and salt and pepper to taste. Bring to the boil, cover and simmer for 20 minutes, stirring occasionally.

Turn the beef mixture into a casserole. Beat 50 g/2 oz of the cheese into the potatoes and spread or pipe over the beef mixture. Sprinkle with the remaining cheese and bake in a preheated oven for 30 minutes or until the topping is browned. Garnish with parsley before serving.

Minced beef and potato pie, Meatballs with spicy tomato sauce

Lamb and apricots with orange dumplings

Metric
2 × 15 ml spoons oil
1 kg neck or breast of
  lamb, trimmed and cut
  into pieces
2 onions, peeled and
  chopped
1 garlic clove, peeled and
  crushed
25 g plain flour
450 ml light chicken stock
1 bay leaf
thin strip of orange rind
225 g dried apricots,
  placed in cold water to
  cover and soaked
  overnight
salt
freshly ground black
  pepper

Orange dumplings:
100 g self-raising flour
pinch of salt
50 g shredded suet
finely grated rind and
  juice of 1 orange

Imperial
2 tablespoons oil
2¼ lb neck or breast of
  lamb, trimmed and cut
  into pieces
2 onions, peeled and
  chopped
1 garlic clove, peeled and
  crushed
1 oz plain flour
¾ pint light chicken stock
1 bay leaf
thin strip of orange rind
8 oz dried apricots,
  placed in cold water to
  cover and soaked
  overnight
salt
freshly ground black
  pepper

Orange dumplings:
4 oz self-raising flour
pinch of salt
2 oz shredded suet
finely grated rind and
  juice of 1 orange

Preparation time: 30 minutes, plus soaking time
Cooking time: 2 hours
Oven: 160°C, 325°F, Gas Mark 3

Heat the oil in a flameproof casserole. Add the meat and fry until lightly browned. Remove the meat to a plate. Add the onions to the pot and cook gently until tender, stir in the garlic and flour, and cook for 3–4 minutes. Add the stock, bay leaf, orange rind, apricots and their soaking liquid, and salt and pepper. Bring gently to the boil.
Return the meat to the casserole, cover and cook in a preheated oven for 1½ hours.
Meanwhile, make the dumplings. Mix together the flour, salt, suet and grated orange rind. Make into a soft dough with the orange juice (if this is not enough liquid, use a little water). Shape into eight dumplings. Remove the casserole lid, place the dumplings over the top and return to the oven. Cook for a further 30 minutes or until the dumplings have risen and are lightly coloured.

Swiss steak

Metric
2 × 15 ml spoons oil
1 onion, peeled and
  chopped
50 g seasoned flour
750 g topside or top rump
  of beef, cubed
1 × 225 g can tomatoes,
  sliced
300 ml bottled or canned
  tomato juice
100 g pearl barley,
  washed
1 × 5 ml spoon chopped
  fresh marjoram or
  1 × 2.5 ml spoon dried
  marjoram
salt
freshly ground black
  pepper
225 g green beans, cut
  into 5 cm lengths
225 g button mushrooms

To garnish:
thin green pepper rings
fried croûtons

Imperial
2 tablespoons oil
1 onion, peeled and
  chopped
2 oz seasoned flour
1½ lb topside or top rump
  of beef, cubed
1 × 8 oz can tomatoes,
  sliced
½ pint bottled or canned
  tomato juice
4 oz pearl barley,
  washed
1 teaspoon chopped
  fresh marjoram or
  ½ teaspoon dried
  marjoram
salt
freshly ground black
  pepper
8 oz green beans, cut
  into 2 inch lengths
8 oz button mushrooms

To garnish:
thin green pepper rings
fried croûtons

Preparation time: 25 minutes
Cooking time: 1¾ hours
Oven: 160°C, 325°F, Gas Mark 3

Heat the oil in a flameproof casserole, add the onion and cook gently until softened. Use the seasoned flour to thoroughly coat the meat. Add the meat to the casserole and brown well. Dust in any remaining seasoned flour and cook for 2 minutes.
Add the tomatoes with their juice and the tomato juice. Bring slowly to the boil, stirring well. Add the pearl barley and marjoram, salt and pepper. Cover and transfer to a preheated oven. Cook for 1¼ hours.
Stir in the green beans and mushrooms and adjust the seasoning. Cover and cook for a further 30 minutes. Garnish with pepper rings and croûtons.

Lamb and apricots with orange dumplings,
Swiss steak, Pot roast of beef

Pot roast of beef

Preparation time: 20 minutes
Cooking time: 1½–2 hours
Oven: 190°C, 375°F, Gas Mark 5

Metric	Imperial
2 × 15 ml spoons oil	*2 tablespoons oil*
1 × 1½ kg joint beef topside	*1 × 3 lb joint beef topside*
1 onion, peeled and finely chopped	*1 onion, peeled and finely chopped*
300 ml beef stock	*½ pint beef stock*
2 × 15 ml spoons soy sauce	*2 tablespoons soy sauce*
2 × 15 ml spoons medium dry sherry	*2 tablespoons medium dry sherry*
1 × 5 ml spoon soft brown sugar	*1 teaspoon soft brown sugar*
1 stick cinnamon	*1 stick cinnamon*
salt	*salt*
freshly ground black pepper	*freshly ground black pepper*
1 × 5 ml spoon arrowroot	*1 teaspoon arrowroot*
sesame seeds, toasted, to garnish	*sesame seeds, toasted, to garnish*

Heat the oil in a flameproof casserole, add the beef and brown on all sides. Add the onion and cook gently until golden. Stir in the stock, soy sauce, sherry, sugar, cinnamon, salt and pepper. Cover and transfer to a preheated oven. Cook for 1½ hours or until the meat is tender.

Place the beef on a board, slice it and arrange the slices on a heated serving dish. Keep hot.

Dissolve the arrowroot in a little cold water, add to the sauce and bring to the boil, stirring. Discard the cinnamon stick and adjust the seasoning. Serve the sauce separately or pour it over the beef, garnish with sesame seeds. Serve with whole baked tomatoes.

Sauerbraten

Metric
4 × 15 ml spoons red wine
    vinegar
250 ml beef stock
1 onion, peeled and finely
    chopped
1 celery stick, thinly
    sliced
1 bay leaf
3 cloves
salt
freshly ground black
    pepper
450 g braising steak,
    trimmed and cut into
    4 pieces
1 × 15 ml spoon oil
2 × 15 ml spoons soft
    brown sugar
4 gingernut biscuits,
    crushed

To garnish
1 dessert apple, cored
    and sliced
caster sugar
butter for frying

Imperial
4 tablespoons red wine
    vinegar
8 fl oz beef stock
1 onion, peeled and finely
    chopped
1 celery stick, thinly
    sliced
1 bay leaf
3 cloves
salt
freshly ground black
    pepper
1 lb braising steak,
    trimmed and cut into
    4 pieces
1 tablespoon oil
2 tablespoons soft brown
    sugar
4 gingernut biscuits,
    crushed

To garnish
1 dessert apple, cored
    and sliced
caster sugar
butter for frying

Preparation time: 10 minutes, plus 48 hours
marinating time
Cooking time: 1¾ hours
Oven: 150°C, 300°F, Gas Mark 2

Mix together the vinegar, stock, onion, celery, bay
leaf, cloves, salt and pepper in a glass bowl. Add the
meat, cover and place in the refrigerator. Leave to
marinate for 48 hours, turning the meat several times
to season it evenly.

Drain the meat, reserving the marinade. Heat the oil
in a flameproof casserole, add the meat and fry over a
brisk heat until browned. Strain the marinade into a
measuring jug and pour 250 ml/8 fl oz over the meat.
Bring to the boil, then cover the casserole and cook
in a preheated oven for 1 hour 35 minutes.

Meanwhile, for the garnish, sprinkle the apple rings
with sugar and fry them lightly in butter until golden
brown. Drain and keep warm.

Transfer the meat to a heated dish and keep hot. Skim
off any fat from the cooking liquid and stir in the
sugar and gingernuts. Bring to the boil. Thin if
necessary with a few spoonfuls of the remaining
marinade and adjust the seasoning. Replace the meat
in the casserole and allow to heat through; do not boil.
Serve garnished with the apple rings.

Beef hedgehog

Metric
450 g minced beef
1 garlic clove, peeled
    and crushed
2 × 15 ml spoons chopped
    fresh parsley
4 × 15 ml spoons cold
    water
1 onion, peeled and
    grated
75 g long-grain rice
1 × 2.5 ml spoon ground
    ginger
salt
freshly ground black
    pepper
1 × 275 g can condensed
    tomato soup
milk

To garnish
potato crisps
chopped fresh parsley

Imperial
1 lb minced beef
1 garlic clove, peeled
    and crushed
2 tablespoons chopped
    fresh parsley
4 tablespoons cold
    water
1 onion, peeled and
    grated
3 oz long-grain rice
½ teaspoon ground
    ginger
salt
freshly ground black
    pepper
1 × 10 oz can condensed
    tomato soup
milk

To garnish
potato crisps
chopped fresh parsley

Preparation time: 10 minutes
Cooking time: 45 minutes
Oven: 180°C, 350°F, Gas Mark 4

Mix together the beef, garlic, parsley, cold water,
onion, rice, ginger, salt and pepper. Work the
mixture very well with your hands; this will lighten
the texture. Form into balls with wet hands and place
in a casserole.

Empty the soup into a small saucepan and thin with
half the soup can of milk. Bring to the boil and pour
over the shaped balls. Cover and cook in a preheated
oven for 45 minutes. Serve garnished with potato
crisps and parsley.

Corned beef chilli

Metric	**Imperial**
450 g corned beef, diced	1 lb corned beef, diced
2 onions, peeled and very finely chopped	2 onions, peeled and very finely chopped
225 g potatoes, peeled, diced and boiled	8 oz potatoes, peeled, diced and boiled
2 × 15 ml spoons chopped fresh parsley	2 tablespoons chopped fresh parsley
150 ml milk	¼ pint milk
2 × 5 ml spoons Worcestershire sauce	2 teaspoons Worcestershire sauce
salt	salt
freshly ground black pepper	freshly ground black pepper
3–4 × 15 ml spoons chilli sauce	3–4 tablespoons chilli sauce
sprigs of watercress, to garnish	sprigs of watercress, to garnish

Preparation time: 10 minutes
Cooking time: 30 minutes
Oven: 180°C, 350°F, Gas Mark 4

Chilli sauce is very hot, so use it cautiously.

Mix together the beef, onions, potato, parsley, milk,
Worcestershire sauce, salt and pepper. Pack into a
greased casserole dish and smooth the top. Spread
the chilli sauce over the top. Cover and cook in a
preheated oven for 20 minutes. Uncover and cook for
a further 10 minutes.
Serve garnished with watercress.

Sauerbraten, Beef hedgehog, Corned beef chilli

Spicy silverside

Metric	Imperial
1 × 1¼ kg joint salted silverside	1 × 2½ lb joint salted silverside
2 large onions, peeled and quartered	2 large onions, peeled and quartered
8 whole cloves	8 whole cloves
2 bay leaves	2 bay leaves
8 black peppercorns	8 black peppercorns
4 large carrots, peeled and thickly sliced	4 large carrots, peeled and thickly sliced
2 turnips, peeled and quartered	2 turnips, peeled and quartered
1–2 parsnips, peeled and sliced (optional)	1–2 parsnips, peeled and sliced (optional)
1 leek, trimmed and sliced	1 leek, trimmed and sliced
1 × 15 ml spoon brown sugar	1 tablespoon brown sugar

Dumplings (optional):	Dumplings (optional):
150 g self-raising flour	6 oz self-raising flour
pinch of salt	pinch of salt
75 g shredded suet	3 oz shredded suet
1 × 5 ml spoon dried mixed herbs	1 teaspoon dried mixed herbs
about 5–6 × 15 ml spoons cold water	about 5–6 tablespoons cold water

Preparation time: 10 minutes
Cooking time: 2–2½ hours

Salted brisket may be used in place of silverside, but increase the cooking time by about 30 minutes.

Soak the joint in cold water for 2 hours, if you do not like a very salty flavour. Drain the joint, place in a saucepan and cover with fresh water. Add all the other ingredients and bring to the boil. Skim off any scum from the surface, then cover the pan and simmer gently for 2–2½ hours or until the beef is tender.
To make dumplings to serve with the beef, sift the flour and salt into a bowl and mix in the suet and herbs. Bind to a softish dough with water, then shape into 8 balls. About 15 minutes before the joint has finished cooking, add the dumplings to the casserole and cover. When cooked, remove the dumplings with a slotted spoon.
Transfer the joint to a heated serving dish. Using a slotted spoon transfer the vegetables and arrange them around the meat with the dumplings. Spoon off any fat from the surface of the cooking liquid and strain some into a jug for a sauce. Serve with boiled or creamed potatoes and a green vegetable.

Devilled steaks

Metric	Imperial
4 steaks (rump, sirloin or quick-fry)	4 steaks (rump, sirloin or quick-fry)
1 garlic clove, peeled and crushed	1 garlic clove, peeled and crushed
1 × 15 ml spoon grated onion	1 tablespoon grated onion
1 × 15 ml spoon French mustard	1 tablespoon French mustard
large pinch of chilli powder	large pinch of chilli powder
1 × 5 ml spoon Worcestershire sauce	1 teaspoon Worcestershire sauce
2 × 15 ml spoons tomato ketchup	2 tablespoons tomato ketchup
salt	salt
freshly ground black pepper	freshly ground black pepper
40 g butter	1½ oz butter
100 g button mushrooms	4 oz button mushrooms

To garnish:	To garnish:
thin carrot strips	thin carrot strips
watercress	watercress

Preparation time: 5 minutes
Cooking time: 5–15 minutes, according to taste

Quick-fry steaks, which are thinner, will take less time to cook than rump or sirloin steaks, and may be grilled or fried in melted butter. Chilli powder, which is very hot, can vary in strength according to the brand used.

Trim the steaks and place them on the rack in the grill pan. Combine the garlic, onion, mustard, chilli powder, Worcestershire sauce, tomato ketchup and salt and pepper to taste and spread half of the mixture over the steaks.
Put the steaks under a moderate grill and cook, allowing 2 minutes each side for a rare steak, 3 minutes for medium or 4–5 minutes for well done. As the steaks are turned over spread them with the remaining devilled mixture.
Meanwhile, melt the butter in a frying pan and gently fry the mushrooms.
Arrange the steaks on a heated serving dish, spoon any pan juices over and surround with the mushrooms. Garnish with strips of carrot and watercress.

Spicy silverside, Devilled steaks

Spiced lamb cassoulet

Metric	Imperial
2 breasts of lamb or 1¼ kg stewing neck of lamb	2 breasts of lamb or 2½ lb stewing neck of lamb
2 × 15 ml spoons dripping or oil	2 tablespoons dripping or oil
2 onions, peeled and sliced	2 onions, peeled and sliced
3 carrots, peeled and sliced	3 carrots, peeled and sliced
1 red pepper, cored, seeded and sliced	1 red pepper, cored, seeded and sliced
1 × 15 ml spoon plain flour	1 tablespoon plain flour
450 ml stock	¾ pint stock
1 × 5 ml spoon dried thyme or 2 × 5 ml spoons fresh thyme	1 teaspoon dried thyme or 2 teaspoons fresh thyme
2 × 15 ml spoons wine vinegar	2 tablespoons wine vinegar
salt	salt
freshly ground black pepper	freshly ground black pepper
1 × 425 g can red kidney beans	1 × 15 oz can red kidney beans
chopped parsley, to garnish	chopped parsley, to garnish

Preparation time: 10 minutes
Cooking time: 2 hours
Oven: 180°C, 350°F, Gas Mark 4

If you prefer, 225 g/8 oz dried red kidney beans may be used in place of the canned variety. Soak them overnight in cold water, then drain. Bring to the boil in fresh water, then boil for 10 minutes. Cover and simmer for 1¼–1½ hours. Add to the casserole, with 150 ml/¼ pint of their cooking liquid.

Trim the lamb of all skin, gristle and excess fat and cut the meat into even-sized pieces or chops. Heat the dripping or oil in a frying pan, add the pieces of lamb and fry until browned on all sides. Remove to a casserole dish.
Add the onions to the pan and fry in the same fat until lightly browned. Add to the casserole with the carrots and red pepper.
Discard all but 1 × 15 ml spoon/1 tablespoon of fat from the pan and stir in the flour followed by the stock, thyme, vinegar and salt and pepper to taste. Drain the beans and add the liquid to the pan. Bring to the boil, stirring well, then pour into the casserole. Cover tightly and cook in a preheated oven for 1 hour.
Stir in the beans, adjust the seasoning and return to the oven. Bake for a further 30–45 minutes or until the lamb is tender. Spoon off any excess fat from the surface of the casserole and sprinkle with parsley.

Braised shoulder of lamb

Metric	Imperial
1 × 1¾ kg shoulder of lamb, boned and rolled	1 × 4 lb shoulder of lamb, boned and rolled
salt	salt
freshly ground black pepper	freshly ground black pepper
1 garlic clove, peeled and crushed (optional)	1 garlic clove, peeled and crushed (optional)
2 × 15 ml spoons dripping or oil	2 tablespoons dripping or oil
2 onions, peeled and thickly sliced	2 onions, peeled and thickly sliced
1 leek, trimmed and sliced	1 leek, trimmed and sliced
4 carrots, peeled and thickly sliced	4 carrots, peeled and thickly sliced
150 ml stock	¼ pint stock
150 ml cider or additional stock	¼ pint cider or additional stock
sprig of fresh rosemary or 1 × 2.5 ml spoon dried rosemary	sprig of fresh rosemary or ½ teaspoon dried rosemary
1 × 5 ml spoon cornflour (optional)	1 teaspoon cornflour (optional)

Preparation time: 10 minutes
Cooking time: about 2½ hours
Oven: 180°C, 350°F, Gas Mark 4

Trim the lamb of excess fat and rub all over with salt, pepper and the garlic. Heat the dripping or oil in a frying pan, add the lamb and fry until sealed and browned all over. Remove from the pan.
Add the vegetables to the pan and fry for a few minutes. Transfer to a casserole just large enough to hold the amount of lamb and vegetables. Place the lamb on the bed of vegetables.
Bring the stock and cider or additional stock to the boil, season with salt, pepper and rosemary, and pour over the lamb.
Cover the casserole and cook in a preheated oven for 2–2½ hours or until the lamb is tender. Adding a little more boiling stock after 1½ hours, if necessary.
Remove the lamb to a heated serving dish and using a slotted spoon surround with the drained vegetables. Spoon off any fat from the cooking juices, discard the sprig of rosemary and serve the juices in a sauceboat. If you prefer a thicker sauce, pour the juices into a small pan and add the cornflour dissolved in a little cold water. Bring to the boil and simmer for 1–2 minutes, stirring.

Spiced lamb cassoulet, Braised shoulder of lamb, Lamb chops in wine with mushrooms

Lamb chops in wine with mushrooms

Preparation time: 10 minutes
Cooking time: 1 hour
Oven: 180°C, 350°F, Gas Mark 4

If the chump chops are very small you may prefer to allow two per person.

Metric
4 lamb chump chops
salt
freshly ground black
  pepper
1 × 15 ml spoon oil
1 onion, peeled and sliced
1 garlic clove, peeled and
  crushed
175 g carrots, peeled and
  diced
100 g button mushrooms,
  halved
150 ml dry white wine
1 bay leaf

To garnish:
tomato slices
chopped parsley

Imperial
4 lamb chump chops
salt
freshly ground black
  pepper
1 tablespoon oil
1 onion, peeled and sliced
1 garlic clove, peeled and
  crushed
6 oz carrots, peeled and
  diced
4 oz button mushrooms,
  halved
¼ pint dry white wine
1 bay leaf

To garnish:
tomato slices
chopped parsley

Trim the chops and season well on both sides with salt and pepper. Heat the oil in a frying pan, add the chops and fry until well browned on both sides. Transfer to a shallow ovenproof dish.

Drain off all but 1 × 15 ml spoon/1 tablespoon fat from the pan, then add the onion, garlic and carrots and fry until soft but not coloured. Add the mushrooms, wine, bay leaf, salt and pepper, and bring to the boil. Pour over the chops.

Cover with a lid or foil and cook in a preheated oven for 45–60 minutes or until the chops are tender. Discard the bay leaf. Garnish with slices of tomato and sprinkle with chopped parsley before serving.

Paprika kidney sauté

Metric	Imperial
12 lamb's kidneys, skinned, halved and cored	12 lamb's kidneys, skinned, halved and cored
25 g seasoned flour	1 oz seasoned flour
40 g butter	1½ oz butter
1 × 15 ml spoon oil	1 tablespoon oil
1 onion, peeled and sliced	1 onion, peeled and sliced
1 red pepper, cored, seeded and chopped	1 red pepper, cored, seeded and chopped
1 × 15 ml spoon paprika	1 tablespoon paprika
450 ml beef stock	¾ pint beef stock
generous dash of Tabasco sauce	generous dash of Tabasco sauce
salt	salt
freshly ground black pepper	freshly ground black pepper

Preparation time: 10 minutes
Cooking time: 25–30 minutes

Coat the kidneys in the seasoned flour, reserving any leftover flour. Melt the butter with the oil in a frying pan, add the onion and red pepper and fry gently until tender but not coloured. Add the kidneys and continue cooking until very well sealed and lightly browned. Stir in the left-over seasoned flour and the paprika, followed by the stock and Tabasco sauce. Bring to the boil, stirring well.

Cover and simmer gently for about 20 minutes or until the kidneys are tender. Adjust the seasoning and serve with freshly boiled rice.

Paprika kidney sauté, Crunchy herb-topped liver, Creamy liver

Crunchy herb-topped liver

Metric	Imperial
8 thick slices of lamb's or pig's liver	8 thick slices of lamb's or pig's liver
salt	salt
freshly ground black pepper	freshly ground black pepper
1 × 425 g can tomatoes	1 × 15 oz can tomatoes
6 × 15 ml spoons dry parsley and thyme or sage and onion stuffing mix	6 tablespoons dry parsley and thyme or sage and onion stuffing mix
2 × 15 ml spoons water	2 tablespoons water
6 streaky bacon rashers, rind removed, halved	6 streaky bacon rashers, rind removed, halved
15 g butter	½ oz butter
fresh parsley, to garnish	fresh parsley, to garnish

Preparation time: 5 minutes
Cooking time: 1 hour
Oven: 190°C, 375°F, Gas Mark 5

Put half the liver slices in a casserole or ovenproof dish and season well with salt and pepper. Cover with the tomatoes, reserving a little of the juice, then sprinkle with half of the stuffing mix. Cover with the remaining liver, pour over the reserved tomato juice and the water and add salt and pepper to taste. Lay the pieces of bacon on top. Sprinkle with the remaining stuffing, dot with the butter and cover the casserole. Cook in a preheated oven for 30 minutes. Remove the lid and return to the oven for a further 20–30 minutes, until the liver is tender and the topping crispy. Garnish with parsley before serving.

Creamy liver

Metric
40 g butter
6 large spring onions,
   trimmed and sliced,
   or 1 medium onion,
   peeled and sliced
1 × 300 g can sweetcorn
   kernels, drained
450 g lamb's liver
   (8 slices)
salt
freshly ground black
   pepper
3 large tomatoes, skinned
   and sliced
2 × 5 ml spoons plain flour
4 × 15 ml spoons stock
   or water
150 ml soured cream
chopped fresh parsley,
   to garnish

Imperial
1½ oz butter
6 large spring onions,
   trimmed and sliced,
   or 1 medium onion,
   peeled and sliced
1 × 11 oz can sweetcorn
   kernels, drained
1 lb lamb's liver
   (8 slices)
salt
freshly ground black
   pepper
3 large tomatoes, skinned
   and sliced
2 teaspoons plain flour
4 tablespoons stock or
   water
¼ pint soured cream
chopped fresh parsley,
   to garnish

Preparation time: 5 minutes
Cooking time: about 15 minutes

Melt 15 g/½ oz of the butter in a saucepan, add the onions and fry gently for 2–3 minutes. Stir in the sweetcorn and continue cooking for 2–3 minutes.
Wipe the liver and season with salt and pepper. Melt the remaining butter in a frying pan, add the liver and fry quickly until well sealed and browned – about 4–5 minutes on each side.
Add the tomatoes to the sweetcorn mixture and allow to heat through but not become mushy. Season well with salt and pepper and spoon on to a heated serving dish. Arrange the cooked liver on top and keep warm. Stir the flour into the drippings in the frying pan and cook for 1 minute. Gradually stir in the stock or water followed by the soured cream over a low heat, then bring to the boil. Simmer for 2 minutes, stirring frequently. Adjust the seasoning, pour over the liver and serve sprinkled with parsley.

Pork fillet in a crust

Preparation time: about 25 minutes
Cooking time: about 1¼ hours
Oven: 220°C, 425°F, Gas Mark 7
　　　180°C, 350°F, Gas Mark 4

Metric
450 g pork fillet
2–3 × 15 ml spoons oil
　or dripping
15 g butter or margarine
1 small onion, peeled and
　finely chopped
4 streaky bacon rashers,
　rind removed, chopped
75 g mushrooms, chopped
1 medium cooking apple,
　peeled, cored and
　chopped
1 × 1.25 ml spoon dried
　mixed herbs
salt
freshly ground black
　pepper
1 × 375 g packet frozen
　puff pastry, thawed
beaten egg, to glaze
1 × 15 ml spoon plain flour
300 ml beef stock
1 × 15 ml spoon tomato
　purée

Imperial
1 lb pork fillet
2–3 tablespoons oil
　or dripping
½ oz butter or margarine
1 small onion, peeled and
　finely chopped
4 streaky bacon rashers,
　rind removed, chopped
3 oz mushrooms, chopped
1 medium cooking apple,
　peeled, cored and
　chopped
¼ teaspoon dried mixed
　herbs
salt
freshly ground black
　pepper
1 × 13 oz packet frozen
　puff pastry, thawed
beaten egg, to glaze
1 tablespoon plain flour
½ pint beef stock
1 tablespoon tomato
　purée

To garnish:
fried apple rings
watercress

To garnish:
fried apple rings
watercress

Cut the pork fillets to about 23 cm/9 inches long, to make an even-sized joint, then tie together into an oblong shape with string. Heat the oil or dripping in a frying pan, add the pork and fry very gently for 15–20 minutes or until well browned all over. Remove from the pan and allow to cool. Reserve the juices in the pan for gravy.

Melt the butter or margarine in a pan, add the onion and bacon and fry until the onion is soft. Add the mushrooms and apple and continue frying for 2–3 minutes. Add the herbs and salt and pepper to taste and leave to cool.

Roll out the dough on a floured surface to a size large enough to enclose the pork. Spread the mushroom mixture down the centre of the pastry. Remove the string and place the pork on top of the mushroom mixture. Wrap the pastry around the pork and seal, dampening the edges with water. Place in a lightly greased baking tin with the seam underneath. Decorate with leaves made from the trimmings, then glaze well with beaten egg.

Cook in a preheated oven for 30 minutes. Reduce the oven temperature and continue cooking for 15–20 minutes. Cover with a sheet of greaseproof paper when the pastry is sufficiently browned.

Meanwhile make the gravy. Stir the flour into the reserved pan juices and cook for 1 minute. Gradually stir in the stock and tomato purée and bring to the boil. Simmer for 2 minutes. Season to taste with salt and pepper.

Place the pork on a heated serving dish, garnish with fried apple rings and watercress and serve with the gravy.

Pork fillet in a crust, Orange glazed bacon,
Pork chops with cheese and pineapple

Orange glazed bacon

Metric
4 bacon chops (2.5 cm
  thick slices of back
  bacon), rind removed
grated rind and juice of
  1 orange
1 × 15 ml spoon clear
  honey

Imperial
4 bacon chops (1 inch
  thick slices of back
  bacon), rind removed
grated rind and juice of
  1 orange
1 tablespoon clear
  honey

To garnish:
orange slices
watercress

To garnish:
orange slices
watercress

Preparation time: 5 minutes
Cooking time: 10–15 minutes

Make deep cuts into the fat of the chops at 2 cm/$\frac{3}{4}$ inch intervals to prevent curling up during cooking and place in a foil-lined grill pan. Combine the orange rind and juice and honey and brush over the chops. Cook under a preheated moderate grill for 2–3 minutes or until beginning to brown. Brush again with the orange glaze and continue cooking until the fat is brown and crispy. Turn the chops over and cook the second side in the same way, glazing twice.
Place 2 orange slices on each chop, brush with the remaining glaze, return to the grill and cook for a further 1–2 minutes. Serve garnished with watercress and with any remaining glaze and the juices from the pan poured over the chops.

Pork chops with cheese and pineapple

Metric
15 g butter
1 onion, peeled and finely
  chopped
1 × 375 g can crushed
  pineapple, partly
  drained
4 pork chops or boneless
  pork slices
salt
freshly ground black
  pepper
75 g mature Cheddar
  cheese, grated
25 g shelled walnuts,
  chopped

Imperial
½ oz butter
1 onion, peeled and finely
  chopped
1 × 13 oz can crushed
  pineapple, partly
  drained
4 pork chops or boneless
  pork slices
salt
freshly ground black
  pepper
3 oz mature Cheddar
  cheese, grated
1 oz shelled walnuts,
  chopped

Preparation time: 5 minutes
Cooking time: about 25 minutes

Melt the butter in a small pan, add the onion and fry gently until soft. Stir in the pineapple and cook for 5 minutes or until the liquid has been absorbed.
Season the chops on both sides with salt and pepper and place in a grill pan. Cook under a preheated moderate heat for about 5 minutes on each side or until well browned. Spoon the pineapple mixture over the chops and return to the grill for a further 4–5 minutes cooking or until the juices run clear when the flesh is pierced with a skewer.
Combine the cheese and walnuts and sprinkle thickly over the pineapple. Return to the grill and cook until lightly browned. Serve at once.

Pot roast stuffed chicken

Metric	Imperial
1 × 1½–1¾ kg oven-ready chicken	1 × 3½–4 lb oven-ready chicken
25 g butter or margarine	1 oz butter or margarine
1 onion, peeled and finely chopped	1 onion, peeled and finely chopped
75 g fresh breadcrumbs	3 oz fresh breadcrumbs
2 × 15 ml spoons chopped fresh parsley	2 tablespoons chopped fresh parsley
1 × 2.5 ml spoon dried thyme	½ teaspoon dried thyme
1 × 1.25 ml spoon grated lemon rind	¼ teaspoon grated lemon rind
50 g salted peanuts, finely chopped	2 oz salted peanuts, finely chopped
salt	salt
freshly ground black pepper	freshly ground black pepper
1 egg yolk	1 egg yolk
lemon juice (optional)	lemon juice (optional)
15 g butter, melted	½ oz butter, melted
300 ml boiling chicken stock, or half stock and half white wine	½ pint boiling chicken stock, or half stock and half white wine
2 × 15 ml spoons double cream (optional)	2 tablespoons double cream (optional)

Preparation time: 20 minutes
Cooking time: 1½ hours
Oven: 180°C, 350°F, Gas Mark 4

Gently ease the skin away from the flesh all over the breast of the chicken, using your hand, and taking care not to tear the skin. Melt the butter or margarine in a pan, add the onion and fry gently until soft. Remove from the heat and stir in the breadcrumbs, parsley, thyme, lemon rind, peanuts and salt and pepper. Mix well and bind together with the egg yolk and a little lemon juice if necessary.

Carefully spread two-thirds of the stuffing in an even layer between the skin and flesh on the breast of the bird, then use the remainder to stuff the neck end. Secure the neck flap, truss the bird and tie the legs together. Place the bird in a deep casserole just large enough to hold it. Season the stock, or stock and wine, with salt and pepper and pour around the bird. Cover and cook in a preheated oven for 1¼ hours.

Remove the lid, baste the bird with the pan juices and return to the oven, uncovered. Cook for a further 15 minutes to brown the breast. Remove the bird to a heated serving dish and garnish with parsley and lemon. Skim any fat from the pan juices and serve. Alternatively, stir in the double cream, after adjusting the seasoning.

Chicken and ham pudding

Metric	Imperial
200 g self-raising flour	8 oz self-raising flour
1 × 2.5 ml spoon salt	½ teaspoon salt
75 g shredded suet	3 oz shredded suet
2 × 15 ml spoons grated onion	2 tablespoons grated onion
about 150 ml cold water	about ¼ pint cold water

Filling:

Metric	Imperial
225 g lean collar bacon, rind removed, chopped	8 oz lean collar bacon, rind removed, chopped
350 g chicken meat, chopped	12 oz chicken meat, chopped
1 onion, peeled and chopped	1 onion, peeled and chopped
1 × 5 ml spoon dried mixed herbs	1 teaspoon dried mixed herbs
100 g mushrooms, chopped	4 oz mushrooms, chopped
salt	salt
freshly ground black pepper	freshly ground black pepper
4 × 15 ml spoons water, cider or white wine	4 tablespoons water, cider or white wine

Preparation time: 20 minutes
Cooking time: 3–3½ hours

To make the suet pastry, sift the flour and salt into a bowl and mix in the suet and onion. Bind to a softish dough with cold water. Reserve one-quarter of the dough for the lid; roll out the remainder to a circle about twice the diameter of the top of a greased 1 litre/ 2 pint pudding basin. Carefully lower the dough into the basin and press lightly to line it evenly without creases or tears.

Mix together the bacon, chicken, onion, herbs, mushrooms and salt and pepper to taste. Spoon into the basin and add the water, cider or wine.

Roll out the reserved dough for a lid. Dampen the edges and place on top of the filling, pressing the edges well together, and trimming off surplus dough. Cover with a piece of buttered greaseproof paper, pleated down the centre, and then cover securely with foil or a pudding cloth.

Put the basin into a saucepan and add enough boiling water to come two-thirds of the way up the side of the basin. Cover and simmer very gently for 3–3½ hours, adding more boiling water as necessary. Remove the coverings and serve the pudding straight from the basin. A parsley sauce may also be served.

Simmered chicken with cheese, Chicken and ham pudding, Pot roast stuffed chicken

Simmered chicken with cheese

Preparation time: 5 minutes
Cooking time: 25–30 minutes

Metric
25 g butter or margarine
1 × 15 ml spoon oil
8 chicken drumsticks
1 onion, peeled and
 chopped
2 × 15 ml spoons plain
 flour
300 ml milk
150 ml chicken stock
salt
freshly ground black
 pepper
pinch of garlic powder
1 × 2.5 ml spoon dried
 thyme
4 × 15 ml spoons single
 cream
75 g mature Cheddar or
 Gruyère cheese, grated
3 × 15 ml spoons fresh
 breadcrumbs
sprigs of fresh parsley or
 green pepper rings, to
 garnish

Imperial
1 oz butter or margarine
1 tablespoon oil
8 chicken drumsticks
1 onion, peeled and
 chopped
2 tablespoons plain
 flour
½ pint milk
¼ pint chicken stock
salt
freshly ground black
 pepper
pinch of garlic powder
½ teaspoon dried
 thyme
4 tablespoons single
 cream
3 oz mature Cheddar or
 Gruyère cheese, grated
3 tablespoons fresh
 breadcrumbs
sprigs of fresh parsley or
 green pepper rings, to
 garnish

Boneless chicken breasts may also be used for this recipe, but reduce the cooking time by about 5 minutes.

Melt the butter or margarine with the oil in a shallow flameproof casserole, add the drumsticks and fry until browned all over. Remove from the pan. Add the onion to the pan and fry in the same fat until soft. Stir in the flour and cook for 1 minute. Gradually stir in the milk and chicken stock and bring to the boil. Season well with salt and pepper, add the garlic powder and thyme and replace the chicken in the pan. Cover and simmer very gently for about 20 minutes, or until the chicken is tender, turning it once or twice. Stir the cream and 50 g/2 oz of the cheese into the sauce, adjust the seasoning and bring back to the boil. Combine the remaining cheese with the breadcrumbs and sprinkle over the chicken. Place the casserole under a preheated hot grill to brown the topping.
Serve from the pan garnished with parsley or rings of green pepper.

Sugar baked bacon

Metric	Imperial
1 × 1½ kg prime collar joint of bacon, boned, rolled and soaked in cold water for 2–4 hours	1 × 3 lb prime collar joint of bacon, boned, rolled and soaked in cold water for 2–4 hours
4 whole cloves	4 whole cloves
1 bay leaf	1 bay leaf
6 × 15 ml spoons demerara sugar	6 tablespoons demerara sugar

Cider sauce:

Metric	Imperial
40 g butter or margarine	1½ oz butter or margarine
1 onion, peeled and thinly sliced	1 onion, peeled and thinly sliced
40 g plain flour	1½ oz plain flour
300 ml cider	½ pint cider
150 ml milk or additional cider	¼ pint milk or additional cider
salt	salt
freshly ground black pepper	freshly ground black pepper

To garnish:

Metric	Imperial
apple slices, dipped in water and lemon juice	apple slices, dipped in water and lemon juice
watercress	watercress

Preparation time: 5 minutes, plus soaking time
Cooking time: about 1¾ hours
Oven: 190°C, 375°F, Gas Mark 5

One of the advantages of a joint of bacon cooked in this way is that it is just as delicious served cold.

Drain the bacon, then weigh and calculate the cooking time: allow 30 minutes per 450 g/1 lb plus 30 minutes over. Place the joint in a saucepan and cover with fresh water. Add the cloves, bay leaf and 2 × 15 ml spoons/2 tablespoons of the sugar and bring to the boil. Cover and simmer for half the total cooking time.
Drain the joint, strip off the skin and place the joint on foil. Score the fat and sprinkle with the remaining sugar. Wrap the foil around the joint and place in a roasting tin. Cook in a preheated oven until 15 minutes before the end of the total cooking time, then fold back the foil to complete the cooking and brown the fat. Meanwhile make the sauce. Melt the butter or margarine in a pan, add the onion and fry until soft. Stir in the flour and cook for 1 minute. Gradually stir in the cider and milk or additional cider and bring to the boil. Simmer for 2 minutes. Season to taste with salt and pepper. Just before serving, stir in 1–2 × 15 ml spoons/1–2 tablespoons of the juices from the joint. Garnish the joint with slices of apple and watercress, and serve with the sauce.

Sweet and sour chicken

Metric	Imperial
4 chicken portions	4 chicken portions
salt	salt
freshly ground black pepper	freshly ground black pepper
2 × 15 ml spoons dripping or oil	2 tablespoons dripping or oil
1 × 200 g can pineapple rings (4 rings)	1 × 7 oz can pineapple rings (4 rings)
2 × 15 ml spoons soy sauce	2 tablespoons soy sauce
1 × 15 ml spoon tomato ketchup	1 tablespoon tomato ketchup
1 × 15 ml spoon wine vinegar	1 tablespoon wine vinegar
1 × 15 ml spoon soft brown sugar	1 tablespoon soft brown sugar
1 onion, peeled and sliced	1 onion, peeled and sliced
1 red or green pepper, cored, seeded and sliced	1 red or green pepper, cored, seeded and sliced
1 × 15 ml spoon plain flour	1 tablespoon plain flour
1 × 425 g can tomatoes	1 × 15 oz can tomatoes
freshly boiled rice, to serve	freshly boiled rice, to serve

Preparation time: 10 minutes
Cooking time: about 1 hour
Oven: 180°C, 350°F, Gas Mark 4

Season the chicken portions all over with salt and pepper. Heat the dripping or oil in a frying pan, add the chicken and fry until well browned all over. Transfer to a casserole.
Drain the pineapple, reserving the syrup; chop two rings and sprinkle over the chicken. Reserve the remaining pineapple for the garnish. Make up the syrup to 150 ml/¼ pint with water. Add the soy sauce, ketchup, vinegar and sugar to the syrup.
Add the onion and red or green pepper to the frying pan and fry in the same fat until tender. Stir in the flour and cook for 1 minute, then add the pineapple syrup mixture and tomatoes and bring to the boil, stirring well. Add salt and pepper to taste and simmer for 2 minutes. Pour over the chicken.
Cover the casserole and cook in a preheated oven for about 45 minutes or until the chicken is tender. Serve with freshly boiled rice and garnish each piece of chicken with half a pineapple ring.

Sugar baked bacon, Sweet and sour chicken

Turkey with piquant avocado sauce

Metric
4 turkey escalopes or slices
    of breast meat
seasoned flour for coating
1 egg, beaten
about 75 g fresh white
    breadcrumbs

Sauce:
3 × 15 ml spoons white
    wine vinegar
1 × 15 ml spoon finely
    chopped onion
1 bay leaf
6 black peppercorns
3 egg yolks
175 g butter, chopped
1 ripe avocado, peeled
    halved and stoned
1 × 15 ml spoon lemon
    juice

40 g butter
4 × 15 ml spoons oil
lemon slices, to garnish

Imperial
4 turkey escalopes or slices
    of breast meat
seasoned flour for coating
1 egg, beaten
about 3 oz fresh white
    breadcrumbs

Sauce:
3 tablespoons white wine
    vinegar
1 tablespoon finely
    chopped onion
1 bay leaf
6 black peppercorns
3 egg yolks
6 oz butter, chopped
1 ripe avocado, peeled
    halved and stoned
1 tablespoon lemon
    juice

1½ oz butter
4 tablespoons oil
lemon slices, to garnish

Preparation time: 15 minutes, plus chilling time
Cooking time: 15 minutes

If the escalopes are thick, place them between two sheets of greaseproof paper and beat with a rolling pin until about 5 mm/¼ inch thick. Dust with seasoned flour, then dip in the beaten egg and coat evenly in breadcrumbs. Chill for at least 15 minutes.
To make the sauce, put the vinegar, onion, bay leaf and peppercorns into a saucepan, bring to the boil and boil until reduced by half. Strain into a heatproof basin and leave to cool.
Beat the egg yolks into the vinegar mixture and place over a pan of gently simmering water. Cook gently until the sauce thickens, stirring constantly. Gradually add the butter, stirring, and continue cooking gently until thick and creamy. Remove from the heat.
Slice half the avocado and brush with a little of the lemon juice. Set aside. Mash the other half thoroughly with the lemon juice, then beat into the sauce until smooth. Keep warm over a pan of hot water.
Melt the butter with the oil in a frying pan, add the escalopes and fry gently for about 5 minutes each side or until golden brown and cooked through. Drain well on kitchen paper and arrange on a heated serving dish.
Spoon a little of the sauce across the escalopes and garnish with slices of lemon and avocado. Serve the remaining sauce in a small bowl.

Turkey goulash

Metric
3 × 15 ml spoons dripping
    or margarine
450–500 g turkey
    casserole meat, cubed
2 onions, peeled and sliced
2 carrots, peeled and
    chopped
1–2 garlic cloves, peeled
    and crushed
1 small green pepper,
    cored, seeded and sliced
1 × 15 ml spoon paprika
2 × 15 ml spoons plain
    flour
2 × 15 ml spoons tomato
    purée
450 ml stock
salt
freshly ground black
    pepper
225 g tomatoes, skinned
    and sliced
soured cream, to serve
    (optional)

Imperial
3 tablespoons dripping
    or margarine
1–1¼ lb turkey casserole
    meat, cubed
2 onions, peeled and sliced
2 carrots, peeled and
    chopped
1–2 garlic cloves, peeled
    and crushed
1 small green pepper,
    cored, seeded and sliced
1 tablespoon paprika
2 tablespoons plain
    flour
2 tablespoons tomato
    purée
¾ pint stock
salt
freshly ground black
    pepper
8 oz tomatoes, skinned
    and sliced
soured cream, to serve
    (optional)

Preparation time: 10 minutes
Cooking time: 1 hour
Oven: 180°C, 350°F, Gas Mark 4

Turkey casserole meat is dark meat, which is available from many supermarkets and delicatessens, but a mixture of boneless dark and white meat or all white meat may also be used for this recipe.

Melt the dripping or margarine in a frying pan, add the turkey meat and fry until well sealed. Transfer to a casserole. Add the onions, carrots, garlic and green pepper to the frying pan and fry gently for about 5 minutes or until soft but not coloured. Stir in the paprika, flour and tomato purée and cook for 1 minute. Gradually stir in the stock and bring to the boil. Season well with salt and pepper, add the tomatoes and pour over the turkey. Mix well.
Cover the casserole and cook in a preheated oven for about 45 minutes or until the turkey is tender. Soured cream may be spooned on to each portion. Serve with noodles, rice or macaroni.

Somerset turkey, Turkey goulash, Turkey with piquant avocado sauce

Somerset turkey

Preparation time: 10 minutes
Cooking time: 1 hour
Oven: 180°C, 350°F, Gas Mark 4

Metric
25 g butter
2 × 15 ml spoons oil
500 g turkey meat, cubed
1 large onion, peeled and
    sliced
1 green pepper, cored,
    seeded and sliced
2 × 15 ml spoons plain
    flour
300 ml cider
300 ml chicken stock
1 × 200 g can sweetcorn
    kernels, drained
100 g mushrooms, sliced
salt
freshly ground black
    pepper
1 large eating apple,
    peeled, cored and sliced
fresh parsley and thyme,
    chopped, to garnish

Imperial
1 oz butter
2 tablespoons oil
1¼ lb turkey meat, cubed
1 large onion, peeled and
    sliced
1 green pepper, cored,
    seeded and sliced
2 tablespoons plain
    flour
½ pint cider
½ pint chicken stock
1 × 7 oz can sweetcorn
    kernels, drained
4 oz mushrooms, sliced
salt
freshly ground black
    pepper
1 large eating apple,
    peeled, cored and sliced
fresh parsley and thyme,
    chopped, to garnish

Melt the butter with the oil in a frying pan, add the turkey meat and fry until lightly browned. Remove to a casserole.

Add the onion and green pepper to the frying pan and fry in the same fat until soft. Stir in the flour and cook for 1 minute. Gradually stir in the cider and stock and bring to the boil, then add the sweetcorn, mushrooms, salt and pepper and pour into the casserole. Cover and cook in a preheated oven for 30 minutes.

Adjust the seasoning, stir in the apple and replace the lid. Return the casserole to the oven for a further 15 minutes cooking or until the turkey is tender. Adjust the seasoning and serve, sprinkled with the fresh herbs.

Fish fingers with tomato and mushroom sauce

Metric	**Imperial**
450 g cod fillets, skinned	1 lb cod fillets, skinned
100 g fresh breadcrumbs	4 oz fresh breadcrumbs
2 × 15 ml spoons chopped fresh parsley	2 tablespoons chopped fresh parsley
2 × 15 ml spoons finely chopped onion	2 tablespoons finely chopped onion
1 garlic clove, peeled and crushed (optional)	1 garlic clove, peeled and crushed (optional)
grated rind of ½ lemon	grated rind of ½ lemon
salt	salt
freshly ground black pepper	freshly ground black pepper
1 egg, beaten	1 egg, beaten
2–3 × 15 ml spoons oil	2–3 tablespoons oil

Sauce:	**Sauce:**
150 ml tomato ketchup	¼ pint tomato ketchup
6 × 15 ml spoons chicken stock	6 tablespoons chicken stock
6 × 15 ml spoons white wine	6 tablespoons white wine
100 g mushrooms, chopped	4 oz mushrooms, chopped
1 garlic clove, peeled and crushed	1 garlic clove, peeled and crushed
lemon slices, to garnish	lemon slices, to garnish

Preparation time: 10 minutes
Cooking time: 20–25 minutes
Oven: 200°C, 400°F, Gas Mark 6

Cut the fish into fingers about 7.5 × 2.5 cm/3 × 1 inches. Combine the breadcrumbs, parsley, onion, garlic, lemon rind and salt and pepper to taste. Dip the pieces of fish into the beaten egg, then coat well in the breadcrumb mixture. Place in a very well oiled baking tin. Cook in a preheated oven for 20–25 minutes until the topping is crispy and the fish cooked through.

Meanwhile make the sauce. Put the tomato ketchup, stock and wine into a pan with salt and pepper and bring to the boil. Cover and simmer for 10 minutes, stirring occasionally. Add the mushrooms and garlic and continue simmering for 5 minutes or until the sauce is thick and smooth. Adjust the seasoning and serve hot with the fish fingers, garnished with lemon.

Cod and mushroom gratiné

Metric	**Imperial**
4 cod steaks or cutlets	4 cod steaks or cutlets
150 ml white wine or cider	¼ pint white wine or cider
300 ml milk	½ pint milk
1 bay leaf	1 bay leaf
salt	salt
freshly ground black pepper	freshly ground black pepper
500 g potatoes, peeled, freshly boiled, mashed and seasoned	1¼ lb potatoes, peeled, freshly boiled, mashed and seasoned
50 g butter	2 oz butter
1 small onion, peeled and chopped	1 small onion, peeled and chopped
100 g mushrooms, sliced	4 oz mushrooms, sliced
40 g plain flour	1½ oz plain flour
40 g mature Cheddar or Gruyère cheese, grated	1½ oz mature Cheddar or Gruyère cheese, grated

Preparation time: 15 minutes
Cooking time: 25 minutes

Put the fish in a pan with the wine or cider, milk, bay leaf and plenty of salt and pepper and poach for about 10 minutes or until tender.

Meanwhile, pipe the potato around the rim of a heated shallow flameproof dish using a large star nozzle. Drain the fish, reserving the cooking liquid, and place in the centre of the dish. Keep warm. Strain the liquid and make it up to 450 ml/¾ pint with milk or water. Melt the butter in a pan, add the onion and fry gently until soft but not coloured. Add the mushrooms and continue cooking for 1–2 minutes. Stir in the flour and cook for 1 minute, then gradually stir in the fish liquid and bring to the boil. Simmer for 2–3 minutes. Adjust the seasoning and pour over the fish. Sprinkle with the cheese.

Place under a moderate grill and cook until the cheese and potato are golden. Serve with peas and tomatoes.

Fish puffs with curry mayonnaise

Preparation time: 10 minutes
Cooking time: 15 minutes

Metric
450 g white fish fillets,
  skinned
1 onion, peeled
1 garlic clove, peeled
  (optional)
50 g fresh white
  breadcrumbs
salt
freshly ground black
  pepper
large pinch of ground
  nutmeg
1 × 15 ml spoon cream
golden breadcrumbs for
  coating
fat for deep frying

Curry mayonnaise:
4 × 15 ml spoons thick
  mayonnaise
2 × 15 ml spoons double
  cream
1 × 2.5 ml spoon curry
  powder (or to taste)
1 × 15 ml spoon chopped
  fresh parsley

To garnish:
mustard and cress
tomatoes

Imperial
1 lb white fish fillets,
  skinned
1 onion, peeled
1 garlic clove, peeled
  (optional)
2 oz fresh white
  breadcrumbs
salt
freshly ground black
  pepper
large pinch of ground
  nutmeg
1 tablespoon cream
golden breadcrumbs for
  coating
fat for deep frying

Curry mayonnaise:
4 tablespoons thick
  mayonnaise
2 tablespoons double
  cream
½ teaspoon curry
  powder (or to taste)
1 tablespoon chopped
  fresh parsley

To garnish:
mustard and cress
tomatoes

Mince the fish, onion and garlic finely, then mix with the fresh breadcrumbs, plenty of salt and pepper, the nutmeg and cream. Shape into balls about the size of a walnut and roll in the golden breadcrumbs. At this stage the puffs can be conveniently refrigerated for several hours.

Heat a pan of deep fat until a cube of bread will brown in about 30 seconds. Fry the puffs a few at a time for about 4 minutes, turning over once or twice, until they are golden brown and cooked through. Drain on kitchen paper and keep warm while frying the remaining batches.

To make the curry mayonnaise, combine all the ingredients with salt and pepper to taste and place in a small serving bowl.

Pile the fish puffs on a heated serving dish, garnish with mustard and cress and wedges of tomato and serve with the sauce.

Variation:
A tomato mayonnaise may be served in place of curry if preferred. To the mayonnaise add 2 × 15 ml spoons/ 2 tablespoons tomato ketchup, a generous dash of Worcestershire sauce, a squeeze of lemon juice and salt and pepper to taste; omit the double cream and curry powder.

Cod and mushroom gratiné, Fish puffs with curry mayonnaise, Fish fingers with tomato and mushroom sauce

Ocean pie

Metric

450 g white fish fillets,
  skinned
175 g soft herring roes
300 ml milk
salt
freshly ground black
  pepper
100 g streaky bacon
  rashers, rind removed,
  chopped and crisply
  fried
6 spring onions, trimmed
  and finely chopped
2 hard-boiled eggs, sliced
25 g butter or margarine
25 g plain flour
50 g mature Cheddar
  cheese, grated
500 g potatoes, peeled,
  freshly boiled and
  mashed

Imperial

1 lb white fish fillets,
  skinned
6 oz soft herring roes
½ pint milk
salt
freshly ground black
  pepper
4 oz streaky bacon
  rashers, rind removed,
  chopped and crisply
  fried
6 spring onions, trimmed
  and finely chopped
2 hard-boiled eggs, sliced
1 oz butter or margarine
1 oz plain flour
2 oz mature Cheddar
  cheese, grated
1¼ lb potatoes, peeled,
  freshly boiled and
  mashed

Preparation time: 15 minutes
Cooking time: about 45 minutes
Oven: 200°C, 400°F, Gas Mark 6

When there is a little more time to spare grilled or fried bacon rolls can be arranged over the pie before serving.

Put the fish, herring roes, milk and plenty of salt and pepper in a pan and poach until tender – about 10 minutes. Drain off the liquid and make it up to 300 ml/½ pint with more milk or water.
Roughly flake the fish, discarding any bones. Roughly chop the roes. Mix the fish and roes with the crispy bacon and the onions. Place in a greased ovenproof dish and cover with the sliced eggs.
Melt the butter or margarine in a pan and stir in the flour. Cook for 1 minute, then gradually stir in the fish cooking liquid over a low heat and bring to the boil. Simmer for 2 minutes. Season with salt and pepper and stir in the cheese until melted. Pour over the eggs.
Pipe a lattice of potato over the sauce and cook in a preheated oven for about 30 minutes or until the top is lightly browned.

Grilled mackerel with mustard sauce

Metric	Imperial
8 mackerel fillets	8 mackerel fillets
25 g butter, melted	1 oz butter, melted
salt	salt
freshly ground black pepper	freshly ground black pepper
4 × 15 ml spoons medium oatmeal	4 tablespoons medium oatmeal

Sauce:

Metric	Imperial
25 g butter or margarine	1 oz butter or margarine
1½ × 15 ml spoons plain flour	1½ tablespoons plain flour
300 ml chicken stock	½ pint chicken stock
1 × 15 ml spoon French mustard	1 tablespoon French mustard
1 × 5 ml spoon made mustard (English)	1 teaspoon made mustard (English)
1 × 5 ml spoon lemon juice	1 teaspoon lemon juice
3 × 15 ml spoons thick mayonnaise	3 tablespoons thick mayonnaise

To garnish:

sprigs of parsley	sprigs of parsley
cucumber slices	cucumber slices

Preparation time: 10 minutes
Cooking time: 20 minutes

Place the mackerel fillets, skin sides down, in the grill pan. Brush with the melted butter and season well with salt and pepper. Sprinkle with the oatmeal. Cook under a preheated moderate grill for about 10 minutes or until the fish is cooked through and the oatmeal lightly browned.

Meanwhile make the sauce. Melt the butter or margarine in a pan, stir in the flour and cook for 1 minute. Gradually stir in the stock over a low heat and bring to the boil. Simmer for 2 minutes. Stir in the mustards, lemon juice and mayonnaise and reheat gently, then pour into a serving jug.

Arrange the mackerel fillets on a heated serving dish and garnish with parsley and cucumber. Serve with the sauce.

Grilled mackerel with mustard sauce, Ocean pie, Stuffed plaice rolls with spinach

Stuffed plaice rolls with spinach

Metric	Imperial
1 × 225 g packet frozen leaf spinach, or 450 g fresh spinach, trimmed	1 × 8 oz packet frozen leaf spinach, or 1 lb fresh spinach, trimmed
salt	salt
freshly ground black pepper	freshly ground black pepper
pinch of ground nutmeg	pinch of ground nutmeg
65 g butter	2½ oz butter
8 plaice fillets	8 plaice fillets
300 ml milk	½ pint milk
4 × 15 ml spoons fresh breadcrumbs	4 tablespoons fresh breadcrumbs
25 g plain flour	1 oz plain flour
2 × 15 ml spoons thick mayonnaise	2 tablespoons thick mayonnaise
2 × 15 ml spoons double cream (optional)	2 tablespoons double cream (optional)
75 g mature Cheddar cheese, grated	3 oz mature Cheddar cheese, grated
watercress, to garnish	watercress, to garnish

Preparation time: 15 minutes
Cooking time: about 50 minutes
Oven: 180°C, 350°F, Gas Mark 4

If very large plaice fillets are available, four will be sufficient.

If using frozen spinach, cook it according to the directions on the packet. Wash and cook the fresh spinach without any extra water for about 10 minutes, until tender. Drain thoroughly and chop roughly. Season with salt and pepper to taste, add the nutmeg and beat in 15 g/½ oz of the butter. Divide the spinach between the plaice fillets and roll each one up neatly. Arrange in a buttered shallow ovenproof dish that will just hold the plaice rolls comfortably. Pour over the milk, season well with salt and pepper and cover with foil or a lid. Cook in a preheated oven for 40–45 minutes or until the fish is tender.

Meanwhile, melt 25 g/1 oz of the butter in a frying pan. Add the breadcrumbs and fry gently until golden brown, stirring constantly. Drain on kitchen paper and set aside.

Drain off the cooking liquid from the fish and reserve. Keep the fish warm. Melt the remaining butter in a saucepan, stir in the flour and cook for 1 minute. Gradually stir in the fish cooking liquid over a low heat and bring to the boil. Simmer for 2 minutes. Stir in the mayonnaise and cream followed by the cheese. Adjust the seasoning and pour over the fish to coat it evenly. Spoon the fried crumbs down the centre of the fish and garnish with watercress.

Seafood gougère

Preparation time: 20 minutes
Cooking time: about 45 minutes
Oven: 220°C, 425°F, Gas Mark 7

Metric	Imperial
50 g butter	2 oz butter
150 ml water	¼ pint water
65 g plain flour	2½ oz plain flour
2 eggs, beaten	2 eggs, beaten
1 × 15 ml spoon chopped fresh parsley	1 tablespoon chopped fresh parsley
2 × 15 ml spoons grated Parmesan cheese	2 tablespoons grated Parmesan cheese
salt	salt
freshly ground black pepper	freshly ground black pepper

Filling:

Metric	Imperial
450 g white fish fillets, skinned	1 lb white fish fillets, skinned
300 ml milk	½ pint milk
1 bay leaf	1 bay leaf
salt	salt
freshly ground black pepper	freshly ground black pepper
40 g butter or margarine	1½ oz butter or margarine
100 g mushrooms, chopped	4 oz mushrooms, chopped
25 g plain flour	1 oz plain flour
1 × 150 g jar mussels, drained	1 × 5 oz jar mussels, drained
50 g peeled prawns (optional)	2 oz peeled prawns (optional)
12 stuffed olives, sliced	12 stuffed olives, sliced

To garnish:

Metric	Imperial
few whole prawns	few whole prawns
sprigs of parsley	sprigs of parsley

To make the choux pastry gougère, melt the butter in the water in a pan and bring to the boil. Sift in the flour all at once and beat until the mixture forms a ball which leaves the sides of the pan clean. Remove from the heat and cool slightly. Gradually beat in the eggs until the mixture becomes smooth and glossy; beat in as much air as possible. (The mixture may not need all of the second egg; it must be firm enough to hold its shape.) Beat in the chopped parsley, Parmesan cheese and salt and pepper.

Spread out the mixture in a hollow ring about 23 cm/ 9 inches wide on a greased baking sheet. Cook in a preheated oven for 35–40 minutes or until well risen, golden brown and firm.

While the gougère is cooking, prepare the filling. Put the fish, milk, bay leaf and plenty of salt and pepper in a pan and poach for about 10 minutes or until tender. Drain off the liquid and make up to 300 ml/ ½ pint with milk. Remove the bay leaf and roughly flake the fish.

Melt the butter or margarine in a pan, add the mushrooms and fry for 1–2 minutes. Stir in the flour and cook for 1 minute, then gradually stir in the cooking liquid and bring to the boil. Simmer for 2 minutes. Season well with salt and pepper and stir in the flaked fish, mussels, prawns and olives. Simmer for 2 minutes. Remove the gougère from the oven and slide on to a heated serving dish. Cut off the top and spoon in the fish filling. Replace the lid and serve at once, garnished with whole prawns and parsley.

Haddock and tomato hotpot

Preparation time: 10 minutes
Cooking time: 1 hour
Oven: 180°C, 350°F, Gas Mark 4

Metric	Imperial
500 g haddock fillets, skinned	1¼ lb haddock fillets, skinned
1 onion, peeled and very finely chopped	1 onion, peeled and very finely chopped
salt	salt
freshly ground black pepper	freshly ground black pepper
1 × 2.5–5 ml spoon dried basil	½–1 teaspoon dried basil
1 × 425 g can tomatoes	1 × 15 oz can tomatoes
750 g potatoes, peeled, par-boiled and sliced	1½ lb potatoes, peeled, par-boiled and sliced
50 g Cheddar cheese, grated	2 oz Cheddar cheese, grated

Lay half the fish in a greased casserole. Sprinkle with half the onion, salt and pepper and a little of the basil, then add half the tomatoes and a layer of sliced potatoes. Repeat with the remainder of the ingredients, except the cheese, finishing with a layer of potatoes. Cover the casserole and cook in a preheated oven for 30 minutes.

Remove the lid, sprinkle with the cheese and return to the oven uncovered. Cook for a further 20–25 minutes or until the potatoes are tender and the topping lightly browned.

Haddock and tomato hotpot, Seafood gougère

Salads and Vegetables

Nowadays salads are not just confined to the warmer weather but have become part of everyday eating. Ingredients which used to appear only in summer are now available for much longer periods, thus making it possible to serve some kind of fresh salad at any time of the year.

Vegetables, raw or cooked, are an important part of a daily diet. Unfortunately they are often overcooked, which makes them soggy and uninteresting. It is better to undercook vegetables so all their flavour, texture and valuable nutrients are retained. Main dishes based on vegetables are an excellent idea; they are cheap and easy to prepare, and will be a delicious surprise for the family.

Onion and cheese flan, Bacon and spinach salad

Bacon and spinach salad

Metric	Imperial
300–350 g fresh spinach leaves	10–12 oz fresh spinach leaves
225 g streaky bacon rashers, rind removed, chopped	8 oz streaky bacon rashers, rind removed, chopped
2 × 15 ml spoons finely chopped or grated onion	2 tablespoons finely chopped or grated onion
2 eating apples, peeled, cored and chopped	2 eating apples, peeled, cored and chopped
2 × 15 ml spoons French Dressing (page 56)	2 tablespoons French Dressing (page 56)
8 hard-boiled eggs	8 hard-boiled eggs
150 ml Cooked Salad Dressing (see right)	¼ pint Cooked Salad Dressing (see right)
6 tomatoes, quartered	6 tomatoes, quartered

Preparation time: 20 minutes

Strip the stalks from the spinach. Wash the leaves thoroughly, dry with kitchen paper and shred. Place in a bowl. Fry the bacon in its own fat in a frying pan until very crispy. Drain on kitchen paper and add to the spinach with the onion. Toss the apples in the French dressing and fold through the spinach mixture. Spoon the salad on to individual plates or one large serving dish.

Place the eggs in the centre of the salad, either whole or halved, and spoon enough of the cooked salad dressing over them to coat completely. Arrange the tomatoes around the edge of the salad and serve. Hand extra salad dressing in a sauceboat.

Cooked salad dressing

Metric	Imperial
1½ × 15 ml spoons plain flour	1½ tablespoons plain flour
1½ × 5 ml spoons sugar	1½ teaspoons sugar
1 × 5 ml spoon dry mustard	1 teaspoon dry mustard
salt	salt
white pepper	white pepper
6 × 15 ml spoons milk	6 tablespoons milk
25 g butter	1 oz butter
1 egg, beaten	1 egg, beaten
3–4 × 15 ml spoons wine or tarragon vinegar	3–4 tablespoons wine or tarragon vinegar
4 × 15 ml spoons oil	4 tablespoons oil

Preparation time: 10 minutes
Cooking time: 5 minutes

Mix together the flour, sugar, mustard and salt and pepper to taste in a small saucepan and gradually stir in the milk. Bring slowly to the boil, stirring, and simmer for 1 minute. Remove from the heat and cool slightly, then beat in the butter followed by the egg. Return to the heat and cook to just below boiling, stirring constantly. Do not allow to boil. Remove from the heat and gradually beat in the vinegar to taste, followed by the oil. Adjust the seasoning. Cover and allow the dressing to cool.
This will keep in an airtight container in the refrigerator for 3–4 days. Shake well before use.
Makes about 150 ml/¼ pint

Onion and cheese flan

Metric	Imperial
200 g wholemeal flour	8 oz wholemeal flour
pinch of salt	pinch of salt
50 g margarine	2 oz margarine
50 g lard	2 oz lard
cold water, to mix	cold water, to mix

Filling:	**Filling:**
25 g butter	1 oz butter
450 g onions, peeled and thinly sliced	1 lb onions, peeled and thinly sliced
salt	salt
freshly ground black pepper	freshly ground black pepper
175 g mature Cheddar cheese, grated	6 oz mature Cheddar cheese, grated

To garnish:	**To garnish:**
cucumber slices	cucumber slices
tomato slices	tomato slices

Preparation time: 15–20 minutes
Cooking time: about 45 minutes
Oven: 200°C, 400°F, Gas Mark 6

To make the pastry, mix together the flour and salt in a bowl and rub in the fats until the mixture resembles fine breadcrumbs. Add sufficient water to mix to a pliable dough. Reserve one quarter of the dough; roll out the remainder and use to line a 20 cm/8 inch flan ring or dish.
Melt the butter in a frying pan, add the onions and fry gently until soft and lightly coloured. Drain well and cool slightly, then spoon into the flan case. Season well with salt and pepper. Cover with the grated cheese. Roll out the reserved dough and cut into strips about 2 cm/¾ inch wide. Lay these over the flan to form a lattice. Trim and secure the ends, dampening with cold water.
Cook in a preheated oven for about 30 minutes or until the pastry is cooked through and the cheese lightly browned. Garnish with slices of cucumber and/or tomato and serve hot or cold with a salad.

Brown rice and vegetable risotto

Metric	Imperial
50 g margarine	2 oz margarine
2 × 15 ml spoons oil	2 tablespoons oil
2 large onions, peeled and sliced	2 large onions, peeled and sliced
175 g carrots, peeled and chopped	6 oz carrots, peeled and chopped
1 bulb fennel, (about 225 g) chopped or 1 garlic clove, peeled and crushed	1 bulb fennel (about 8 oz) chopped or 1 garlic clove, peeled and crushed
225 g brown rice	8 oz brown rice
600 ml stock	1 pint stock
1 bay leaf	1 bay leaf
salt	salt
freshly ground black pepper	freshly ground black pepper
1 medium aubergine (about 225 g), diced	1 medium aubergine (about 8 oz), diced
100 g mushrooms, sliced	4 oz mushrooms, sliced
100 g frozen peas	4 oz frozen peas
grated Parmesan cheese, to serve	grated Parmesan cheese, to serve

To garnish:	To garnish:
tomato slices	tomato slices
fresh parsley	fresh parsley

Preparation time: 10 minutes
Cooking time: about 1 hour

Melt the margarine with the oil in a large heavy-based frying pan, add the onions, carrots, fennel or garlic, and fry gently for 10 minutes without browning, stirring frequently. Stir in the rice and cook for 3–4 minutes. Add the stock, bay leaf and salt and pepper to taste and bring to the boil, stirring occasionally. Cover and simmer for 15 minutes.

Add the aubergine and mushrooms and stir well. Cover the pan and continue simmer for 15 minutes, stirring occasionally. Stir in the peas with a little boiling water if all the liquid has been absorbed. Continue cooking for a further 5–10 minutes or until the rice is tender and all the liquid has been absorbed. Adjust the seasoning and discard the bay leaf.

Turn on to a hot serving dish and garnish with slices of tomato and parsley. Serve with grated Parmesan cheese and a green salad.

Variations:

A risotto has almost endless variations: courgettes, fresh or canned tomatoes, garlic, runner or French beans, nuts, peppers and pre-soaked pulses are other suggestions, amending the cooking time if necessary.

Peanut and mortadella salad

Metric	Imperial
450 g white cabbage, cored and finely shredded	1 lb white cabbage, cored and finely shredded
4 spring onions, sliced	4 spring onions, sliced
100–175 g salted peanuts	4–6 oz salted peanuts
225 g Mortadella sausage, sliced and cut into thin strips	8 oz Mortadella sausage, sliced and cut into thin strips
1–2 bunches watercress	1–2 bunches watercress
3 hard-boiled eggs, quartered	3 hard-boiled eggs, quartered

French Dressing:	French Dressing:
150 ml oil	¼ pint oil
3 × 15 ml spoons wine vinegar	3 tablespoons wine vinegar
1 × 15 ml spoon lemon juice	1 tablespoon lemon juice
salt	salt
freshly ground black pepper	freshly ground black pepper
1 × 2.5 ml spoon made mustard	½ teaspoon made mustard
1 × 2.5–5 ml spoon caster sugar	½–1 teaspoon caster sugar
1 garlic clove, peeled and crushed (optional)	1 garlic clove, peeled and crushed (optional)

Preparation time: 10–15 minutes

Mix together the white cabbage, spring onions, peanuts and Mortadella in a bowl. Spoon on to a flat dish and garnish around the edge with small bunches of watercress and quarters of hard-boiled egg.

To make the dressing, put all the ingredients, with salt and pepper to taste, into a screw-topped jar and shake well until emulsified. Add 4–5 × 15 ml spoons/ 4–5 tablespoons of the dressing to the salad and toss well. (Store the left-over dressing in the jar, shaking well before using.)

Variation:

In place of salted peanuts use shelled walnuts, roughly chopped or whole, or lightly toasted split almonds.

Peanut and mortadella salad, Brown rice and vegetable risotto, Macaroni and frankfurter salad

Macaroni and frankfurter salad

Preparation time: 10 minutes
Cooking time: 15 minutes

This dish can be served hot or cold.

Metric	Imperial
225 g short-cut macaroni	*8 oz short-cut macaroni*
salt	*salt*
12 frankfurters or	*12 frankfurters or*
chipolata sausages	*chipolata sausages*
5–6 × 15 ml spoons French	*5–6 tablespoons French*
Dressing (see left)	*Dressing (see left)*
freshly ground black	*freshly ground black*
pepper	*pepper*
1 small green pepper,	*1 small green pepper,*
cored, seeded and	*cored, seeded and*
chopped (optional)	*chopped (optional)*
3–4 spring onions, sliced	*3–4 spring onions, sliced*
2 tomatoes, roughly	*2 tomatoes, roughly*
chopped	*chopped*
50–75 g raisins	*2–3 oz raisins*
fresh parsley, to garnish	*fresh parsley, to garnish*

Following the instructions on the packet cook the macaroni in boiling salted water until just tender. Meanwhile, either heat the frankfurters in boiling water or follow the cooking instructions on the can or packet. Alternatively grill or fry the chipolatas. Cut the frankfurters or chipolatas into 1 cm/½ inch slices and keep warm.

Drain the cooked macaroni, rinse under hot water and drain again very thoroughly. Immediately toss the hot macaroni in the French dressing and add the frankfurters or chipolatas, salt and pepper to taste, and all the remaining ingredients. Mix well.

Garnish and serve immediately for a hot dish, or leave until cold in a covered bowl, then garnish with parsley before serving.

Baked eggs on peppers

Metric
2 × 15 ml spoons oil
2 onions, peeled and
  thinly sliced
1 large red pepper, cored,
  seeded and sliced
2 green peppers, cored,
  seeded and sliced
100 g mushrooms, sliced
4 tomatoes, skinned and
  sliced
salt
freshly ground black
  pepper
garlic powder (optional)
8 eggs

Imperial
2 tablespoons oil
2 onions, peeled and
  thinly sliced
1 large red pepper, cored,
  seeded and sliced
2 green peppers, cored,
  seeded and sliced
4 oz mushrooms, sliced
4 tomatoes, skinned and
  sliced
salt
freshly ground black
  pepper
garlic powder (optional)
8 eggs

Preparation time: 10 minutes
Cooking time: 30 minutes
Oven: 220°C, 425°F, Gas Mark 7

Heat the oil in a frying pan, add the onions and fry gently until soft. Add the peppers and continue frying until these are tender but not browned. Stir in the mushrooms, tomatoes, salt, pepper and garlic powder to taste. Cover and simmer gently for 5 minutes until soft.
Divide the pepper mixture between four individual ovenproof dishes or turn into a large shallow ovenproof dish. Break the eggs and place on top of the pepper mixture. Cook in a preheated oven for 10–12 minutes or until the eggs are just set. Serve immediately with crusty bread or rolls and butter.

Variation:
The eggs can be lightly beaten together, stirred into the pepper mixture and then lightly cooked in a pan until the mixture becomes 'scrambled'. This tastes delicious but it is not as attractive as baking the eggs.

Courgettes and tomatoes provençal

Metric
2 × 15 ml spoons oil
1 onion, peeled and sliced
2 garlic cloves, peeled and
  crushed
1 × 15 ml spoon tomato
  purée
1 × 15 ml spoon water
1 × 5 ml spoon dried basil
salt
freshly ground black
  pepper
750 g courgettes, trimmed
  and cut into sticks
450 g tomatoes, skinned
  and sliced
40 g fresh breadcrumbs
20 g butter

Imperial
2 tablespoons oil
1 onion, peeled and sliced
2 garlic cloves, peeled and
  crushed
1 tablespoon tomato
  purée
1 tablespoon water
1 teaspoon dried basil
salt
freshly ground black
  pepper
1½ lb courgettes, trimmed
  and cut into sticks
1 lb tomatoes, skinned
  and sliced
1½ oz fresh breadcrumbs
¾ oz butter

Preparation time: 10 minutes
Cooking time: 1¼ hours
Oven: 200°C, 400°F, Gas Mark 6

Heat the oil in a pan, add the onion and garlic and fry gently until the onion is golden brown. Stir in the tomato purée, water, basil and salt and pepper to taste and remove from the heat.
Place half the courgettes in a flameproof casserole, cover with half the tomatoes and then all the onion mixture. Add the rest of the courgettes and tomatoes. Cover and cook in a preheated oven for 1 hour, or until the courgettes are tender.
Remove the lid and sprinkle with the breadcrumbs and dot with butter. Place under a preheated moderate grill and cook until the topping is well browned and crispy. Serve with plain boiled rice or as an accompaniment to grilled chops or sausages.

Spinach and cheese pancakes

Metric
100 g plain flour
pinch of salt
1 egg
250–275 ml milk
lard or oil for frying

Filling:
450 g fresh spinach,
  trimmed and finely
  chopped or 250 g
  packet frozen chopped
  spinach, thawed
salt
40 g butter
100 g cottage cheese
100 g mature Cheddar
  cheese, grated
2 hard-boiled eggs,
  chopped
freshly ground black
  pepper

Sauce:
25 g butter or margarine
25 g plain flour
300 ml milk
1 × 2.5 spoon made
  mustard
50 g mature Cheddar
  cheese, grated
4 × 15 ml spoons single
  cream
salt
freshly ground black
  pepper

Imperial
4 oz plain flour
pinch of salt
1 egg
½ pint milk
lard or oil for frying

Filling:
1 lb fresh spinach,
  trimmed and finely
  chopped or 8 oz
  packet frozen chopped
  spinach, thawed
salt
1½ oz butter
4 oz cottage cheese
4 oz mature Cheddar
  cheese, grated
2 hard-boiled eggs,
  chopped
freshly ground black
  pepper

Sauce:
1 oz butter or margarine
1 oz plain flour
½ pint milk
½ teaspoon made
  mustard
2 oz mature Cheddar
  cheese, grated
4 tablespoons single
  cream
salt
freshly ground black
  pepper

Preparation time: about 20 minutes
Cooking time: about 50 minutes
Oven: 220°C, 425°F, Gas Mark 7

If cooked pancakes are stacked on a plate and covered with foil or film they may be stored in the refrigerator for 2–3 days before use. Do not fill until required.

To make the batter, sift the flour and salt into a bowl, make a well in the centre and drop in the egg. Add half the milk and beat to a smooth batter, gradually adding the remaining milk.
Put 1 × 5 ml spoon/1 teaspoon lard or oil into an 18 cm/7 inch frying pan and heat the pan thoroughly over a low heat. When the pan is hot pour off the excess fat or oil. Quickly pour in enough batter to coat the bottom of the pan thinly, tilting the pan to cover the bottom evenly. Increase the heat slightly and cook until the underside of the pancake is golden brown and the batter set on the top. Turn over and cook the other side. Slip the pancake on to a plate and keep warm. Repeat making 8 pancakes in all.
To make the filling, cook the spinach in boiling salted water for 5 minutes. Drain well pressing out all the water with a potato masher. Melt the butter in a pan, add the spinach and fry gently for a few minutes. Stir in the cheeses, eggs and salt and pepper to taste and cook gently for 2–3 minutes. Divide the filling between the pancakes, placing it in the centre. Fold over the 2 sides of the pancake and roll up carefully to make a parcel. Place in a buttered shallow casserole and keep the pancakes hot.
To make the sauce, melt the butter or margarine in a pan, stir in the flour and cook for 1 minute. Gradually stir in the milk over a low heat and bring to the boil. Simmer for 2 minutes, then add the mustard, half the cheese, the cream and salt and pepper to taste. Stir until the cheese has melted. Pour the sauce over the pancakes, sprinkle with the remaining cheese and cook in a preheated oven for 20–30 minutes, or until lightly browned. Serve hot with baked tomatoes.

Baked eggs on peppers, Courgettes and tomatoes provençal, Spinach and cheese pancakes

Cottage cheese salad

Metric
450 g cottage cheese
1 × 7.5 cm piece cucumber, diced
225 g dates, stoned
350 g white cabbage or Chinese leaves, cored and shredded
2 large carrots, peeled and coarsely grated
4 spring onions, chopped or 1 × 15 ml spoon grated onion
2 red eating apples, cored and chopped
4 × 15 ml spoons French Dressing (page 56)
lettuce leaves
parsley sprigs, to garnish

Imperial
1 lb cottage cheese
1 × 3 inch piece cucumber, diced
8 oz dates, stoned
12 oz white cabbage or Chinese leaves, cored and shredded
2 large carrots, peeled and coarsely grated
4 spring onions, chopped or 1 tablespoon grated onion
2 red eating apples, cored and chopped
4 tablespoons French Dressing (page 56)
lettuce leaves
parsley springs, to garnish

Preparation time: 15 minutes

If using Chinese leaves for this recipe a few whole leaves may be used in place of the bed of lettuce leaves.

Put the cottage cheese and cucumber into a bowl. Reserve four dates for the garnish; roughly chop the remainder and mix with the cottage cheese. Combine the cabbage or Chinese leaves, carrots and onions. Dip the apples in the French dressing, then fold into the cabbage mixture.
Arrange a bed of lettuce leaves on a flat serving dish and top with the cabbage mixture, keeping it fairly flat. Spoon the cottage cheese mixture across the centre and garnish with the reserved whole dates and parsley sprigs.

Tuna bean salad

Metric	Imperial
225 g frozen broad beans, cooked and cooled	8 oz frozen broad beans, cooked and cooled
1 × 425 g can red kidney beans, drained and rinsed under cold running water	1 × 15 oz can red kidney beans, drained and rinsed under cold running water
1 × 200 g can tuna fish, drained and roughly flaked	1 × 7 oz can tuna fish, drained and roughly flaked
2 × 15 ml spoons chopped fresh chives	2 tablespoons chopped fresh chives
1 × 5 cm piece cucumber, diced	1 × 2 inch piece cucumber, diced
4 celery sticks, sliced	4 celery sticks, sliced
1 eating apple, quartered, cored and chopped	1 eating apple, quartered, cored and chopped
4–6 × 15 ml spoons French Dressing (page 56)	4–6 tablespoons French Dressing (page 56)
grated rind of ½ lemon	grated rind of ½ lemon
lettuce leaves (optional)	lettuce leaves (optional)

To garnish:	To garnish:
lemon slices	lemon slices
cucumber slices	cucumber slices

Preparation time: 15 minutes

This salad, without the lettuce, will keep in a cool place for several hours before serving.

Put the broad beans and kidney beans in a bowl with the tuna fish, chives, cucumber and celery. Toss the apple in the French dressing with the lemon rind added. Mix thoroughly with the rest of the salad ingredients and serve in a salad bowl. If prefered the salad may be arranged on a bed of crisp lettuce. Garnish with lemon and cucumber slices.

Variation:

Use 175 g/6 oz dried, red kidney beans instead of canned. Soak the beans overnight, drain and cook them in unsalted boiling water for 2–2½ hours until well cooked.

Red bean and carrot salad

Metric	Imperial
1 × 200 g can sweetcorn kernels, drained	1 × 7 oz can sweetcorn kernels, drained
1 × 425 g can red kidney beans, drained	1 × 15 oz can red kidney beans, drained
1 × 15 ml spoon finely chopped onion or spring onion	1 tablespoon finely chopped onion or spring onion
225–350 g carrots, peeled, diced and cooked	8–12 oz carrots, peeled, diced and cooked
4 × 15 ml spoons French Dressing (page 56)	4 tablespoons French Dressing (page 56)
salt	salt
freshly ground black pepper	freshly ground black pepper
lettuce leaves	lettuce leaves

Preparation time: 10 minutes

Mix together all the ingredients, except the lettuce, seasoning to taste with salt and pepper. Spoon on to a bed of lettuce to serve.

Sweetcorn and bean-sprout salad

Metric	Imperial
1 × 300 g can sweetcorn kernels, drained	1 × 11 oz can sweetcorn kernels, drained
1 × 300 g can bean sprouts, drained or 225 g fresh bean sprouts, blanched for 1 minute and drained	1 × 11 oz can bean sprouts, drained or 8 oz fresh bean sprouts, blanched for 1 minute and drained
8 spring onions, chopped	8 spring onions, chopped
4 × 15 ml spoons French Dressing (page 56)	4 tablespoons French Dressing (page 56)
1 × 15 ml spoon soy sauce	1 tablespoon soy sauce
salt	salt
freshly ground black pepper	freshly ground black pepper
spinach leaves, torn into pieces	spinach leaves, torn into pieces

Preparation time: about 8 minutes

Mix together all the ingredients, except the spinach, seasoning to taste with salt and pepper. Line a salad bowl with spinach and spoon the corn salad on top.

Clockwise from the left: Cottage cheese salad, Red bean and carrot salad, Tuna bean salad, Sweetcorn and bean-sprout salad

Cauliflower crisp

Metric	Imperial
1 cauliflower, broken into florets	1 cauliflower, broken into florets
salt	salt
65 g margarine	2½ oz margarine
1 onion, peeled and thinly sliced	1 onion, peeled and thinly sliced
100 g mushrooms, sliced	4 oz mushrooms, sliced
50 g plain flour	2 oz plain flour
600 ml milk	1 pint milk
1 × 5 ml spoon made mustard	1 teaspoon made mustard
175 g mature Cheddar cheese, grated	6 oz mature Cheddar cheese, grated
freshly ground black pepper	freshly ground black pepper
1 small packet potato crisps, roughly crushed	1 small packet potato crisps, roughly crushed

Preparation time: 15 minutes
Cooking time: 35–40 minutes
Oven: 200°C, 400°F, Gas Mark 6

Cook the cauliflower in boiling salted water until just tender, then drain thoroughly. Meanwhile, melt the margarine in a saucepan and gently fry the onion until soft. Stir in the mushrooms and cook for a further 1 minute. Stir in the flour and cook for 1 minute, then gradually stir in the milk over a low heat. Bring to the boil and simmer for 2 minutes. Remove from the heat and stir in the mustard, 100 g/4 oz of the cheese, and salt and pepper to taste. Place the cauliflower in a shallow casserole and pour the sauce over. Mix the crisps with the remaining cheese and sprinkle over the cauliflower. Cook in a preheated oven for about 20 minutes or until the cheese topping is melted and lightly browned.

Variation:

100 g/4 oz streaky bacon rashers, rind removed, chopped and crisply fried, may be mixed with the cheese and crisps.

Bean and carrot hotpot

Metric	Imperial
2 × 15 ml spoons oil	2 tablespoons oil
4 celery sticks, sliced	4 celery sticks, sliced
2 large onions, peeled and sliced	2 large onions, peeled and sliced
500 g carrots, peeled and sliced	1¼ lb carrots, peeled and sliced
1 × 425 g can cannellini beans	1 × 15 oz can cannellini beans
salt	salt
freshly ground black pepper	freshly ground black pepper
1 × 5 ml spoon dried basil or marjoram (optional)	1 teaspoon dried basil or marjoram (optional)
500 g potatoes, peeled and thinly sliced	1¼ lb potatoes, peeled and thinly sliced
150 ml stock	¼ pint stock
chopped fresh parsley, to garnish	chopped fresh parsley, to garnish

Preparation time: 10 minutes
Cooking time: 2 hours
Oven: 180°C, 350°F, Gas Mark 4
      200°C, 400°F, Gas Mark 6

Heat the oil in a frying pan, add the celery and onions and fry gently until tender and lightly coloured. Place half the celery and onions in a casserole. Cover with half the carrots then add the beans (including their liquid) and salt and pepper to taste. Sprinkle with the herbs. Cover with the remaining carrots, then the celery and onion mixture and finally the sliced potatoes. Pour the stock into the casserole. Cover the casserole tightly and cook in a preheated oven for 1¼ hours. Remove the lid and increase the oven temperature. Cook for a further 30 minutes or until the potatoes are lightly browned. Sprinkle with parsley and serve hot with a green vegetable or a salad.

Potato layer

Metric
1 kg potatoes, peeled
salt
1 × 312 g can sweetcorn
    kernels with peppers,
    drained
4 hard-boiled eggs,
    quartered or sliced
4 large tomatoes,
    skinned and sliced
50 g butter or margarine
50 g plain flour
600 ml milk or stock
1½ × 5 ml spoons dried
    mixed herbs
1 × 5 ml spoon dry
    mustard
100 g Cheddar cheese,
    grated
freshly ground black
    pepper

Imperial
2 lb potatoes, peeled
salt
1 × 11 oz can sweetcorn
    kernels with peppers,
    drained
4 hard-boiled eggs,
    quartered or sliced
4 large tomatoes,
    skinned and sliced
2 oz butter or margarine
2 oz plain flour
1 pint milk or stock
1½ teaspoons dried
    mixed herbs
1 teaspoon dry
    mustard
4 oz Cheddar cheese,
    grated
freshly ground black
    pepper

Preparation time: 15 minutes
Cooking time: about 1 hour
Oven: 200°C, 400°F, Gas Mark 6

Cook the potatoes in boiling salted water until almost tender. Drain, then slice. Arrange half the slices in a casserole. Cover first with the sweetcorn, then with the eggs, tomatoes and finally the remaining potatoes.
Melt the butter or margarine in a saucepan, stir in the flour and cook for 1 minute. Gradually stir in the milk or stock over a low heat. Bring to the boil and simmer for 2 minutes. Stir in the herbs, mustard, 75 g/3 oz of the cheese, and salt and pepper to taste. Pour over the potatoes and sprinkle with the remaining cheese. Cook in a preheated oven for about 40 minutes, or until well browned on top. Serve hot with a green vegetable or salad.

Variation:
Fry 1 large onion, peeled and chopped, in 1 × 15 ml spoon/1 tablespoon oil until soft and add as a layer after the sweetcorn.

Cauliflower crisp, Bean and carrot hotpot, Potato layer

Curry and spice chicken salad

Metric
225 g long-grain rice
salt
1 × 5 ml spoon turmeric
1 × 15 ml spoon oil
1 large onion, peeled and
 chopped
2 carrots, peeled and
 chopped
1–2 × 5 ml spoons mild
 curry powder
large pinch each of ground
 ginger, ground allspice
 and ground cinnamon
50 g sultanas
1 small green pepper,
 cored, seeded and cut
 into strips
225–350 g cooked chicken
 meat, cut into strips
 (or any other cooked
 meat)
6 × 15 ml spoons thick
 mayonnaise
3 × 15 ml spoons single or
 double cream
freshly ground black
 pepper

To garnish:
slices of banana, dipped in
 lemon juice
watercress

Imperial
8 oz long-grain rice
salt
1 teaspoon turmeric
1 tablespoon oil
1 large onion, peeled and
 chopped
2 carrots, peeled and
 chopped
1–2 teaspoons mild curry
 powder
large pinch each of ground
 ginger, ground allspice
 and ground cinnamon
2 oz sultanas
1 small green pepper,
 cored, seeded and cut
 into strips
8–12 oz cooked chicken
 meat cut into strips
 (or any other cooked
 meat)
6 tablespoons thick
 mayonnaise
3 tablespoons single or
 double cream
freshly ground black
 pepper

To garnish:
slices of banana, dipped in
 lemon juice
watercress

Preparation time: 15 minutes
Cooking time: 15 minutes

Cook the rice in plenty of boiling salted water with the turmeric added until just tender. Drain, rinse under cold water and drain again very thoroughly.
Heat the oil in a frying pan, add the onion and carrots and fry gently until soft but not coloured. Stir in the curry powder and spices and cook for 1–2 minutes. Remove from the heat and leave to cool.
Mix together the rice, sultanas, green pepper and chicken in a bowl. Beat the mayonnaise, cream and salt and pepper to taste with the curried onion mixture and fold through the chicken mixture. Turn into a serving bowl and garnish with slices of banana and watercress.

Jellied tomato ring

Metric
450 ml tomato juice
4 × 5 ml spoons powdered
 gelatine
225 g tomatoes, skinned
 and chopped
1 × 15 ml spoon grated
 onion
2 × 15 ml spoons finely
 chopped celery
1 × 2.5 ml spoon
 Worcestershire sauce
1 × 15 ml spoon wine
 vinegar
salt
freshly ground black
 pepper

Filling:
1 × 15 ml spoon creamed
 horseradish
grated rind of ½ lemon
6 × 15 ml spoons
 mayonnaise
1–2 × 15 ml spoons lemon
 juice
350 g cooked chicken
 meat, cut into thin
 strips
25 g flaked almonds,
 toasted
lettuce leaves, to garnish

Imperial
¾ pint tomato juice
4 teaspoons powdered
 gelatine
8 oz tomatoes, skinned
 and chopped
1 tablespoon grated
 onion
2 tablespoons finely
 chopped celery
½ teaspoon Worcestershire
 sauce
1 tablespoon wine
 vinegar
salt
freshly ground black
 pepper

Filling:
1 tablespoon creamed
 horseradish
grated rind of ½ lemon
6 tablespoons mayonnaise

1–2 tablespoons lemon
 juice
12 oz cooked chicken
 meat, cut into thin
 strips
1 oz flaked almonds,
 toasted
lettuce leaves, to garnish

Preparation time: 20 minutes, plus time for the jelly to set

Put all but 3–4 × 15 ml spoons/3–4 tablespoons of the tomato juice in a bowl. Use the remainder to dissolve the gelatine in a heatproof basin over a pan of hot water. Stir the dissolved gelatine into the rest of the tomato juice with the tomatoes, onion, celery, Worcestershire sauce, vinegar, and salt and pepper to taste. Pour the mixture into a greased 750–900 ml/ 1¼–1½ pint ring mould and chill until set.
To make the filling, gradually beat the horseradish and lemon rind into the mayonnaise followed by the lemon juice. Add salt and pepper to taste and fold in the chicken strips and almonds.
Invert the tomato ring on to a serving dish and surround with lettuce leaves. Spoon the chicken mixture into the centre of the ring and serve.

Chinese style salad

Preparation time: 15 minutes
Cooking time: about 10 minutes

Metric
350–450 g bean sprouts,
  blanched and drained
3 × 15 ml spoons French
  Dressing (page 56)
2 × 15 ml spoons soy sauce
2 large carrots, peeled and
  cut into thin sticks
1 green pepper, cored,
  seeded, cut into strips,
  blanched and drained
1 bunch of spring onions,
  cut into strips
¼ cucumber, diced
omelette made from
  2 eggs, cooled and cut
  into strips
12 thin slices belly pork
  (about 450 g)
watercress or spring
  onions, to garnish

Imperial
12 oz–1 lb bean sprouts,
  blanched and drained
3 tablespoons French
  Dressing (page 56)
2 tablespoons soy sauce
2 large carrots, peeled and
  cut into thin sticks
1 green pepper, cored,
  seeded, cut into strips,
  blanched and drained
1 bunch of spring onions,
  cut into strips
¼ cucumber, diced
omelette made from
  2 eggs, cooled and cut
  into strips
12 thin slices belly pork
  (about 1 lb)
watercress or spring
  onions, to garnish

Put the bean sprouts in a bowl and toss in the dressing and soy sauce. Leave to go cold. Add the carrots, green pepper, spring onions and cucumber and mix well.
Stir the omelette strips gently into the salad. Season the pork slices and cook under a preheated moderate grill for about 10 minutes on each side or until cooked through and crispy. Either leave the slices whole or cut them into pieces.
Arrange the salad in a serving dish with the pork on top and garnish with watercress or spring onions.

Curry and spice chicken salad, Jellied tomato ring, Chinese style salad with crispy grilled pork

Savoury vegetable pie

Preparation time: 20 minutes
Cooking time: about 1 hour
Oven: 200°C, 400°F, Gas Mark 6

Metric
50 g plain flour, sifted
150 g wholemeal flour
pinch of salt
2 × 5 ml spoons mild curry
  powder (optional)
50 g butter or margarine
50 g lard
about 3 × 15 ml spoons
  water
beaten egg or milk, to
  glaze

Imperial
2 oz plain flour, sifted
6 oz wholemeal flour
pinch of salt
2 teaspoons mild curry
  powder (optional)
2 oz butter or margarine
2 oz lard
about 3 tablespoons
  water
beaten egg or milk, to
  glaze

Filling:
1 small leek trimmed and
  sliced
salt
25 g butter
1 × 15 ml spoon oil
1 medium onion, peeled
  and sliced
1 small red pepper, cored,
  seeded and chopped
100 g celery, sliced
50 g mushrooms, sliced
2 × 5 ml spoons plain flour
1 × 200 g can tomatoes
1 × 15 ml spoon chopped
  fresh parsley
large pinch of garlic
  powder (optional)
freshly ground black
  pepper

Filling:
1 small leek, trimmed and
  sliced
salt
1 oz butter
1 tablespoon oil
1 medium onion, peeled
  and sliced
1 small red pepper, cored,
  seeded and chopped
4 oz celery, sliced
2 oz mushrooms, sliced
2 teaspoons plain flour
1 × 7 oz can tomatoes
1 tablespoon chopped
  fresh parsley
large pinch of garlic
  powder (optional)
freshly ground black
  pepper

Cheese Sauce:
25 g butter or margarine
25 g plain flour
300 ml milk
50 g Cheddar cheese,
  grated
1 × 2.5 ml spoon made
  mustard

parsley sprigs, to garnish

Cheese Sauce:
1 oz butter or margarine
1 oz plain flour
½ pint milk
2 oz Cheddar cheese,
  grated
½ teaspoon made
  mustard

parsley sprigs, to garnish

To make the pastry, mix the flours with the salt and curry powder in a bowl. Rub in the fats until the mixture resembles fine breadcrumbs. Add sufficient water to mix to a pliable dough. Cover and leave to rest or chill while making the filling.

Blanch the leek in boiling salted water for 5 minutes, then drain. Melt the butter with the oil in a saucepan, add the onion, red pepper and celery and fry gently until soft but not coloured. Add the mushrooms and continue frying for 1–2 minutes. Stir in the flour and cook for 1 minute, then add the tomatoes. Bring to the boil, stirring. Simmer for 2 minutes, then remove from the heat. Stir in the leeks, parsley, garlic powder and salt and pepper to taste and leave to cool.

Roll out two-thirds of the dough and use to line a 20 cm/8 inch shallow pie dish or plate. Spoon in the filling. Roll out the remaining dough for a lid. Dampen the edges, position the lid on top and press well together. Trim the edges, then crimp and glaze with beaten egg or milk. Decorate with leaves made from the dough trimmings and glaze again. Cook in a preheated oven for about 40 minutes or until golden brown.

Meanwhile, make the cheese sauce. Melt the butter or margarine in a pan, stir in the flour and cook for 1 minute. Gradually stir in the milk over a low heat and bring to the boil. Simmer for 2 minutes. Stir in the cheese, mustard, salt and pepper. Garnish the pie with parsley and serve with the cheese sauce.

Variation:
Add 1 × 15 ml spoon/1 tablespoon grated Parmesan cheese to the pastry in place of the curry powder.

Braised red cabbage with pork

Metric

1 × 15 ml spoon oil
225 g lean belly pork,
  rind removed, chopped
1 large onion, peeled and
  thinly sliced
750 g red cabbage, cored
  and shredded
2 × 15 ml spoons brown
  sugar
3 × 15 ml spoons wine
  vinegar
3 × 15 ml spoons water
salt
freshly ground black
  pepper
1 large cooking apple,
  peeled, cored and
  chopped
eating apple slices, dipped
  in lemon juice, to
  garnish

Imperial

1 tablespoon oil
8 oz lean belly pork,
  rind removed, chopped
1 large onion, peeled and
  thinly sliced
1½ lb red cabbage, cored
  and shredded
2 tablespoons brown
  sugar
3 tablespoons wine
  vinegar
3 tablespoons water
salt
freshly ground black
  pepper
1 large cooking apple,
  peeled, cored and
  chopped
eating apple slices, dipped
  in lemon juice, to
  garnish

Preparation time: 10 minutes
Cooking time: 1¾ hours
Oven: 160°C, 325°F, Gas Mark 3

Heat the oil in a flameproof casserole, add the pork and fry gently, until lightly coloured. Add the onion and continue frying for 3 to 4 minutes, stirring frequently. Add the cabbage, sugar, vinegar, water, salt and pepper to taste and mix well. Cook for 5 minutes. Stir in the cooking apple.

Cover the casserole and cook in a preheated oven for 1 hour. Give the cabbage a good stir, replace the lid and return to the oven for a further 30 minutes cooking. Adjust the seasoning and serve garnished with apple.

Braised red cabbage with pork, Savoury vegetable pie

Puddings and Desserts

There is usually at least one member of the family who has a sweet tooth, while there may also be someone counting calories. Whichever the case care must be taken to see that children eat plenty of fresh fruit or fruity puddings and not too much sugar, cream or stodgy food, which will not only harm their teeth but may also be an early factor leading to overweight. Long cold days are soon forgotten when there is a steamed fruit pudding or tempting apple pie on the table, while home-made ice cream, soufflés and cheesecakes are just ideal for for warm sunny days or a special dinner. Some consideration for the cook is necessary too, with dishes which do not need to be watched over whilst they are cooking or those which can be prepared and produced chilled at a later stage being particularly helpful. Recipes which are especially quick and easy to make are denoted by a Q symbol followed by the number of minutes it takes to prepare and cook them.

Gingered grape cheesecake, Baked apples with marzipan

Baked apples with marzipan

Metric
4 cooking apples
50–75 g bought marzipan
4 × 15 ml spoons cranberry
    sauce or jelly
4 × 15 ml spoons water
4–6 × 15 ml spoons
    demerara sugar
grated rind of ½ lemon

Imperial
4 cooking apples
2–3 oz bought marzipan
4 tablespoons cranberry
    sauce or jelly
4 tablespoons water
4–6 tablespoons demerara
    sugar
grated rind of ½ lemon

Preparation time: 10 minutes
Cooking time: 40–60 minutes
Oven: 190°C, 375°F, Gas Mark 5

Some varieties of apples cook much faster than others and some tend to burst if over cooked, so check their progress towards the end of the cooking time.

Remove the cores from the apples, make a cut around the centre of the skin and stand the apples in an oven-proof dish. Fill the cores with marzipan and top each apple with 1 × 15 ml spoon/1 tablespoon of cranberry sauce or jelly. Pour the water round the apples and sprinkle with the sugar and lemon rind. Cook un-covered, in a preheated oven for 40–60 minutes until the apples are just tender. Serve with cream or plain unsweetened yogurt.

Variation:
In place of marzipan stuff the apples with a mixture of 50–75 g/2–3 oz sultanas and the grated rind of 1 orange and replace cranberry sauce with orange marmalade.

Gingered grape cheesecake

Metric
50 g butter
150 g gingernuts, crushed
350 g cottage cheese
75 g full fat soft cheese,
    softened
grated rind of 1 lemon
50 g caster sugar
2 × 15 ml spoons lemon
    juice
2 × 15 ml spoons single
    cream or top of the
    milk
2 × 5 ml spoons powdered
    gelatine
1 × 15 ml spoon water
225 g green grapes, halved
    and pipped

Apricot glaze:
2 × 15 ml spoons apricot
    jam
1 × 15 ml spoon water

Imperial
2 oz butter
5 oz gingernuts, crushed
12 oz cottage cheese
3 oz full fat soft cheese,
    softened
grated rind of 1 lemon
2 oz caster sugar
2 tablespoons lemon
    juice
2 tablespoons single
    cream or top of the
    milk
2 teaspoons powdered
    gelatine
1 tablespoon water
8 oz green grapes, halved
    and pipped

Apricot glaze:
2 tablespoons apricot
    jam
1 tablespoon water

Preparation time: 15 minutes, plus chilling time

Melt the butter in a pan and stir in the gingernuts. Press into the bottom of an 18–19 cm/7–7½ inch loose-bottomed cake tin or flan ring. Chill until set. Liquidize or sieve the cottage cheese until it is smooth. Beat in the cream cheese, followed by the lemon rind, sugar, lemon juice and cream or milk. Dissolve the gelatine in the water in a heatproof basin over a pan of hot water, then stir into the cheese mixture. Pour over the crumb base in the tin and chill until set.
To serve, remove the cheesecake carefully from the tin or ring. Decorate the top with the grapes. Dissolve the apricot jam in the water in a small pan and brush over the top of the grapes.

Rhubarb and ginger cobbler

Preparation time: 10 minutes
Cooking time: about 45 minutes
Oven: 200°C, 400°F, Gas Mark 6

Metric
750 g rhubarb, trimmed
and cut into 2.5 cm
pieces
150 ml water
sugar, to taste
3–4 pieces stem ginger,
chopped or 25 g
crystallized ginger,
chopped

Scone topping:
150 g self-raising flour
1 × 5 ml spoon ground
ginger
40 g butter or margarine
40 g caster or soft brown
sugar
5–6 × 15 ml spoons milk
1 × 15 ml spoon demerara
sugar

Imperial
1½ lb rhubarb, trimmed
and cut into 1 inch
pieces
¼ pint water
sugar, to taste
3–4 pieces stem ginger,
chopped or 1 oz
crystallized ginger,
chopped

Scone topping:
6 oz self-raising flour
1 teaspoon ground
ginger
1½ oz butter or margarine
1½ oz caster or soft brown
sugar
5–6 tablespoons milk
1 tablespoon demerara
sugar

Put the rhubarb in a saucepan with the water and bring to the boil. Cover and simmer gently until tender but not mushy. Sweeten to taste and stir in the chopped stem or crystallized ginger. Two-thirds fill a pie dish or casserole with the rhubarb, to allow for the topping.

To make the topping, sift the flour and ginger into a bowl and rub in the fat until the mixture resembles breadcrumbs. Stir in the caster or brown sugar and add sufficient milk to mix to a soft dough. Roll out the dough on a floured surface to about 1 cm/½ inch thick and cut into 4 cm/1½ inch rounds. Arrange the rounds in an overlapping circle around the edge of the pie dish over the rhubarb. Brush the dough rounds with milk and sprinkle with the demerara sugar. Bake in a preheated oven for about 30 minutes or until the topping is well risen and golden brown. Serve hot.

Variation:
Any stewed fruit or combination of fruits can be used for a cobbler and the scone topping may be flavoured to complement the fruit.

Rhubarb and ginger cobbler, Baked orange soufflé, Pear and almond tart

Baked orange soufflé

Metric	Imperial
50 g butter	2 oz butter
50 g plain flour	2 oz plain flour
300 ml lukewarm milk	½ pint lukewarm milk
50 g caster sugar	2 oz caster sugar
grated rind of 2 oranges	grated rind of 2 oranges
3 eggs, separated	3 eggs, separated
1 egg white	1 egg white

Orange Sauce:	**Orange Sauce:**
juice of 2 large oranges	juice of 2 large oranges
25 g caster sugar	1 oz caster sugar
grated rind of ½ orange (optional)	grated rind of ½ orange (optional)
1½–2 × 5 ml spoons cornflour	1½–2 teaspoons cornflour
1 × 15 ml spoon water	1 tablespoon water
sifted icing sugar for dredging	sifted icing sugar for dredging

Preparation time: 10 minutes
Cooking time: 45 minutes
Oven: 190°C, 375°F, Gas Mark 5

Melt the butter in a pan, stir in the flour and cook for 1 minute. Gradually stir in the milk over a low heat and bring slowly to the boil, stirring to give a very thick sauce. Simmer gently for 1–2 minutes, then remove from the heat and allow to cool slightly.
Beat the sugar and orange rind into the sauce, followed by the egg yolks. Whisk the 4 egg whites until stiff and fold carefully and evenly through the mixture. Turn into a buttered 1–1.25 litre/2–2½ pint soufflé dish (or straight-sided ovenproof dish). Bake in a preheated oven for 35–40 minutes or until well risen, browned and firm to the touch. Do not open the oven door during cooking or the soufflé will sink.
Meanwhile make the sauce. Put the orange juice in a small pan with the sugar and orange rind, and bring to the boil, stirring to dissolve the sugar. Dissolve the cornflour in the water, add a little sauce to the cornflour, then stir it into the sauce in the pan. Simmer for 2 minutes, stirring well. Dredge the top of the soufflé with icing sugar and serve immediately, with the orange sauce.

Variations:
Replace the orange rind in the soufflé with lemon or grapefruit rind. Use 1 × 5 ml spoon/1 teaspoon vanilla or almond essence in place of the orange rind.
Dissolve 2–3 × 5 ml spoons/2–3 teaspoons instant coffee powder in the milk and omit the orange rind.
Melt 50 g/2 oz plain chocolate in the milk and omit or halve the quantity of orange rind.

Pear and almond tart

Metric	Imperial
125 g plain flour	5 oz plain flour
pinch of salt	pinch of salt
75 g butter or margarine	3 oz butter or margarine
1½ × 5 ml spoons caster sugar	1½ teaspoons caster sugar
1 egg yolk	1 egg yolk
about 1 × 15 ml spoon water	about 1 tablespoon water

Filling:	**Filling:**
1 × 425 g can pear halves, drained	1 × 15 oz can pear halves, drained
75 g butter or margarine	3 oz butter or margarine
75 g caster sugar	3 oz castor sugar
1 egg (sizes 5, 6), beaten	1 egg (sizes 5, 6), beaten
40 g self-raising flour, sifted	1½ oz self-raising flour, sifted
50 g ground almonds	2 oz ground almonds
few drops of almond essence	few drops of almond essence
15 g flaked almonds	½ oz flaked almonds
15 g glacé cherries, chopped (optional)	½ oz glacé cherries, chopped (optional)
1 × 15 ml spoon demerara sugar or coffee sugar crystals	1 tablespoon demerara sugar or coffee sugar crystals

Preparation time: 15 minutes
Cooking time: about 40 minutes
Oven: 190°C, 375°F, Gas Mark 5

To make the pastry, sift the flour and salt into a bowl and rub in the fat until the mixture resembles breadcrumbs. Mix together the sugar and the egg yolk and add to the flour mixture with sufficient water to mix to a pliable dough. Roll out and use to line a shallow 19–20 cm/7½–8 inch square tin.
Drain and cut the pears into quarters if they are large and arrange them in the pastry case. Cream the butter or margarine with the caster sugar until the mixture is light and fluffy and pale in colour. Beat in the egg followed by the flour, ground almonds and essence. Spread the mixture roughly over the pears. The fruit need not be completely covered as the mixture will rise in baking. Sprinkle with the flaked almonds and cherries, if using, and demerara or coffee sugar. Bake in a preheated oven for about 30 minutes or until the filling is well risen, firm to the touch and golden.
Serve hot or cold with cream, or make a sauce by thickening the pear juice with 1 × 15 ml spoon/1 tablespoon arrowroot; bring to the boil stirring, and simmer for 2–3 minutes until clear.

Variations:
Use other canned fruits such as cherries or apricots.

Steamed apple and apricot pudding

Metric	Imperial
100 g dried apricots, soaked in water overnight	4 oz dried apricots, soaked in water overnight
350 g cooking apples, peeled, cored and sliced	12 oz cooking apples, peeled, cored and sliced
2 × 15 ml spoons granulated sugar	2 tablespoons granulated sugar
100 g soft (tub) margarine	4 oz soft (tub) margarine
100 g caster sugar	4 oz caster sugar
2 eggs	2 eggs
100 g self-raising flour	4 oz self-raising flour
1 × 2.5 ml spoon baking powder	½ teaspoon baking powder

Preparation time: 15 minutes, plus soaking time
Cooking time: 2 hours

It is important that soft margarine is used for this one-stage sponge cake mixture.

Drain the apricots and chop them roughly, then put into a bowl with the apples and granulated sugar and mix well.
Place the soft margarine, caster sugar and eggs in another mixing bowl. Sift in the flour and baking powder and beat the sponge mixture together thoroughly for 2 minutes. Grease a 1.2–1.5 litre/2–2½ pint pudding basin. Pour about one-third of the sponge mixture in the bottom. Cover with half of the fruit mixture, then spread a second layer of the sponge mixture over the fruit. Add the rest of the fruit and top with the remaining sponge mixture.
Cover the basin with a piece of buttered foil, making a pleat across the centre of the foil to allow the pudding to rise, and secure tightly around the edge of the basin with string. Place in a large saucepan and add boiling water to come halfway up the side of the basin.
Cover and simmer gently for 1¾–2 hours, adding more boiling water to the pan if necessary. Turn out the pudding and serve with cream or custard.

Bread, butter and apple pudding, Steamed apple and apricot pudding, Fruit pancakes with apricot sauce

Bread, butter and apple pudding

Metric	Imperial
450 g cooking apples, peeled, cored and sliced	1 lb cooking apples, peeled, cored and sliced
4 × 15 ml spoons chunky marmalade	4 tablespoons chunky marmalade
4–5 slices bread (brown or white), buttered	4–5 slices bread (brown or white), buttered
75 g raisins or sultanas	3 oz raisins or sultanas
75 g demerara sugar	3 oz demerara sugar
2 eggs	2 eggs
450 ml milk	¾ pint milk
pinch of ground cinnamon	pinch of ground cinnamon

Preparation time: 10 minutes, plus 20–30 minutes to allow the mixture to stand
Cooking time: about 1 hour
Oven: 200°C, 400°F, Gas Mark 6

Place just over half the apples in a buttered fairly shallow ovenproof dish. Spread the marmalade on the buttered bread and use half to cover the apples. Sprinkle with half the raisins or sultanas and 2 × 15 ml spoons/2 tablespoons of the sugar.
Layer the remaining apples, bread and raisins or sultanas in this way, without the sugar. Beat the eggs and milk together and pour into the dish. Leave to stand for 20–30 minutes.
Sprinkle with the cinnamon and the remaining sugar and bake in a preheated oven for about 1 hour or until well risen and golden brown. Serve hot or cold with cream or custard.

Fruit pancakes with apricot sauce

Metric	**Imperial**
75 g dried apricots, soaked in 300 ml water overnight	3 oz dried apricots, soaked in ½ pint water overnight
2 × 15 ml spoons medium sherry (optional)	2 tablespoons medium sherry (optional)
grated rind of ½ lemon	grated rind of ½ lemon
25 g sugar	1 oz sugar

Pancakes:	**Pancakes:**
100 g plain flour	4 oz plain flour
pinch of salt	pinch of salt
1 egg	1 egg
250–275 ml milk	½ pint milk
50–75 g currants	2–3 oz currants
lard for frying	lard for frying
caster sugar for dredging	caster sugar for dredging

Preparation time: 20–25 minutes, plus soaking time
Cooking time: 15 minutes

First make the sauce. Increase the apricot soaking liquid to 300 ml/½ pint with water and place in a saucepan with the apricots, sherry and lemon rind. Bring to the boil and simmer gently for 10–15 minutes or until the apricots are tender. Liquidize or sieve to a smooth purée and return the sauce to the pan with the sugar. Heat, stirring, until the sugar has dissolved. Remove from the heat and serve hot or cold.

To make the pancakes, sift the flour and salt into a bowl and make a well in the centre. Break the egg into the well and add a little of the milk. Beat to a smooth batter, gradually adding the rest of the milk. Stir in the currants.

Melt a knob of the lard in a small frying pan and pour in just enough batter to cover the base of the pan, making sure a few currants are in the pancake. Cook for 1–2 minutes until lightly browned then turn the pancake over carefully and cook until the second side is evenly browned. Fold into four, place on a serving dish and keep warm while making 7 more pancakes in the same way. Sprinkle lightly with caster sugar and serve with some of the sauce spooned over the pancakes and the rest in a small bowl.

Chocolate meringue gâteau

Metric	*Imperial*
3 egg whites	3 egg whites
175 g caster sugar	6 oz caster sugar

Filling:

Filling:	*Filling:*
6 × 15 ml spoons milk	6 tablespoons milk
40 g caster sugar	1½ oz caster sugar
40 g plain chocolate, broken into pieces	1½ oz plain chocolate, broken into pieces
1 × 2.5 ml spoon cornflour	½ teaspoon cornflour
2 egg yolks	2 egg yolks
100 g butter, preferably unsalted	4 oz butter, preferably unsalted
about 100 g green grapes, halved and pipped or 2 kiwi fruit, peeled and sliced	about 4 oz green grapes, halved and pipped or 2 kiwi fruit, peeled and sliced
½ chocolate flake bar, crushed, to decorate	½ chocolate flake bar, crushed, to decorate

Preparation time: 20 minutes
Cooking time: about 2 hours
Oven: 150°C, 300°F, Gas Mark 2

Any other soft fruit may be used to decorate this gâteau to suit the season.

Line two baking sheets with non-stick silicone paper. Draw an 18 cm/7 inch circle on one, and a 15 cm/6 inch circle and a 12.5 cm/5 inch circle on the other. Whisk the egg whites until very stiff and dry, then gradually whisk in the sugar, making sure the meringue becomes stiff again between each addition of sugar. Spread or pipe the meringue evenly inside the three circles. Bake in a preheated oven for about 1 hour or until firm. Turn off the heat and leave in the oven until quite cold.
To make the filling, put the milk, sugar and chocolate into a heatproof basin over a pan of gently simmering water and heat until the chocolate melts. Beat the cornflour and egg yolks together. Stir in a little of the chocolate mixture, then stir this into the rest of the chocolate mixture in the bowl. Cook gently, stirring, until the custard coats the back of the spoon. Remove from the heat, cover and cool, but do not chill.
Cream the butter until soft, then gradually beat in the chocolate custard. Use most of the filling to sandwich the meringue circles together, adding the grapes or slices of kiwi fruit around the edge of each meringue circle. Spread the remainder of the filling over the top meringue circle, then sprinkle liberally with chocolate. Decorate with grapes or kiwi fruit.
Serves 4–6

Black Forest cherry cake

Metric	*Imperial*
3 eggs (sizes 1, 2)	3 eggs (sizes 1, 2)
110 g caster sugar	4½ oz caster sugar
75 g plain flour	3 oz plain flour
1 × 15 ml spoon cocoa powder	1 tablespoon cocoa powder
1 × 425 g can black or Morello cherries	1 × 15 oz can black or Morello cherries
2 × 5 ml spoons arrowroot	2 teaspoons arrowroot
300 ml double or whipping cream	½ pint double or whipping cream
2 × 15 ml spoons Kirsch, Cointreau or brandy (optional)	2 tablespoons Kirsch, Cointreau or brandy (optional)
1 chocolate flake bar or chocolate curls, to decorate	1 chocolate flake bar or chocolate curls, to decorate

Preparation time: 20 minutes
Cooking time: 20 minutes
Oven: 190°C, 375°F, Gas Mark 5

Grease and line a 20 cm/8 inch round deep cake tin. Whisk the eggs and sugar in a heatproof basin placed over a pan of hot water until the mixture is thick and pale in colour and the whisk leaves a trail when lifted. (If using an electric mixer no heat is needed.) Remove from the heat and continue whisking until cool. Sift the flour and cocoa together twice and fold lightly and evenly through the whisked mixture. Pour into the prepared tin and bake in a preheated oven for about 20 minutes or until well risen and firm to the touch. Turn on to a wire rack to cool.
Drain the cherries, reserving 150 ml/¼ pint of the can juice. Put the juice in a small pan with the arrowroot. Bring slowly to the boil, stirring, and simmer until thick and clear. Cool.
Halve the cherries, removing the stones, and stir them into the sauce. Whip the cream until stiff.
Cut the cake into three layers, and place the bottom layer on a plate. Cover first with a thin layer of cream then half the cherry mixture. Add the second layer of cake, sprinkle with the liqueur or brandy and spread with a little more cream and the remaining cherry mixture. Add the top cake layer and spread with a thin layer of cream. Put the remaining cream into a piping bag fitted with a star nozzle. Pipe a wheel design on top of the cake, finishing each 'spoke' with a whirl. Decorate with pieces of chocolate flake bar or curls. Leave for at least 2 hours (if possible) before serving.

Black Forest cherry cake, Chocolate meringue gâteau

Lemon and lime soufflé

Metric

3 eggs, separated
175 g caster sugar
grated rind and juice of
  1 large lemon
grated rind and juice of
  1 lime
1 × 15 ml spoon powdered
  gelatine
2 × 15 ml spoons water
150 ml whipping cream

To decorate:
whipped cream
slices of lime or blanched
  pistachio nuts

Imperial

3 eggs, separated
6 oz caster sugar
grated rind and juice of
  1 large lemon
grated rind and juice of
  1 lime
1 tablespoon powdered
  gelatine
2 tablespoons water
¼ pint whipping cream

To decorate:
whipped cream
slices of lime or blanched
  pistachio nuts

Preparation time: about 20 minutes, plus chilling time

When limes are unavailable use 2 large lemons and increase the sugar to 225 g/8 oz.

To prepare the soufflé dish: place a double strip of greased greaseproof paper or foil around a 600 ml/1 pint soufflé dish to stand 2.5–4 cm/1–1½ inches above the rim, and secure with string.
Place the egg yolks in a warmed bowl with the sugar, fruit rinds and strained juices. Whisk until very thick and creamy and the whisk leaves a trail. (This process can be hastened by placing the bowl over a pan of gently simmering water.)
Dissolve the gelatine in the water in a basin over a pan of hot water, cool slightly and stir into the egg mixture. Whip the cream until it is thick but not too stiff. Whisk the egg whites until stiff. Fold first the whipped cream and then the egg whites into the mixture. Pour into the prepared dish and chill thoroughly until set. Before serving carefully remove the paper and decorate with cream and slices of lime or pistachio nuts.
Serves 4–6

Blackcurrant and apple mousse, Lemon and lime soufflé, Grapefruit chiffon pie

Blackcurrant and apple mousse

Metric
225 g blackcurrants
450 g cooking apples,
    peeled, cored and sliced
about 100 g sugar
2 × 5 ml spoons powdered
    gelatine
2 × 15 ml spoons water
150 ml plain unsweetened
    yogurt
2 egg whites
toasted almonds or
    blackcurrants, to
    decorate

Imperial
8 oz blackcurrants
1 lb cooking apples,
    peeled, cored and sliced
about 4 oz sugar
2 teaspoons powdered
    gelatine
2 tablespoons water
¼ pint plain unsweetened
    yogurt
2 egg whites
toasted almonds or
    black currants, to
    decorate

Preparation time: 10 minutes, plus chilling time
Cooking time: 25 minutes

Put the blackcurrants into a saucepan and barely cover with water. Bring to the boil, then cover and simmer gently for 10 minutes. Add the apples and continue simmering for 10–15 minutes or until the fruit is soft and pulpy. Sweeten to taste. Cool slightly, then liquidize the fruit to a purée and rub it through a sieve to remove all pips. Leave to cool completely.
Dissolve the gelatine in the water in a heatproof basin over a pan of hot water, then stir into the fruit purée. Fold the yogurt into the fruit purée. Whisk the egg whites until very stiff and fold into the mixture. Pour into a serving bowl and chill until set.
Decorate with toasted almonds or blackcurrants.
Serves 4–6

Variations:
Blackberries, redcurrants, gooseberries, rhubarb or plums may be used in place of blackcurrants.

Grapefruit chiffon pie

Metric
65 g butter or margarine
175 g sweet biscuits (e.g.
    digestive), crushed
1 × 525 g can grapefruit
    segments
2 eggs, separated
75 g caster sugar
2 × 5 ml spoons powdered
    gelatine

Imperial
2½ oz butter or margarine
6 oz sweet biscuits (e.g.
    digestive), crushed
1 × 1 lb 3 oz can
    grapefruit segments
2 eggs, separated
3 oz caster sugar
2 teaspoons powdered
    gelatine

To decorate:
whipped cream
toasted flaked almonds

To decorate:
whipped cream
toasted flaked almonds

Preparation time: 20–30 minutes, plus chilling time

Melt the butter or margarine in a pan and stir in the biscuit crumbs. Press the crumb mixture over the bottom and sides of a greased 20 cm/8 inch flan ring placed on a flat plate, or a loose-bottomed flan tin. Chill while making the filling.
Drain the grapefruit, reserving 150 ml/¼ pint of the can juice. Put the juice in a heatproof basin placed over a pan of hot water and beat in the egg yolks and sugar. Cook gently, stirring, until the mixture thickens, then remove from the heat. Dissolve the gelatine in 1 × 15 ml spoon/1 tablespoon of the grapefruit juice or water in another small heatproof basin over the pan of hot water, then stir into the egg yolk mixture. Cool until the consistency of unbeaten egg white.
Chop the grapefruit segments and stir into the gelatine mixture. Whisk the egg whites until stiff and fold through the grapefruit mixture. Pour into the crumb case and chill until set.
To serve, remove the flan ring and decorate the pie with whipped cream and toasted almonds.

Variations:
Other canned fruits may be used in place of the grapefruit.

Strawberry tartlets

Metric	Imperial
100 g self-raising flour	4 oz self-raising flour
pinch of salt	pinch of salt
25 g butter	1 oz butter
25 g hard margarine	1 oz hard margarine
15 g lard	½ oz lard
2 × 5 ml spoons caster sugar	2 teaspoons caster sugar
about 1 × 15 ml spoon beaten egg	about 1 tablespoon beaten egg

Filling:

Metric	Imperial
175 g full fat soft cheese	6 oz full fat soft cheese
grated rind of ½ lemon	grated rind of ½ lemon
25 g caster sugar	1 oz caster sugar
2–3 × 5 ml spoons lemon juice	2–3 teaspoons lemon juice

Topping:

Metric	Imperial
225 g strawberries, hulled and halved if large	8 oz strawberries, hulled and halved if large
2 × 15 ml spoons redcurrant jelly	2 tablespoons redcurrant jelly
1 × 15 ml spoon water	1 tablespoon water

Preparation time: 10 minutes, plus chilling time
Cooking time: 20 minutes
Oven: 200°C, 400°F, Gas Mark 6

To make the pastry, sift the flour and salt into a bowl and rub in the fats until the mixture resembles breadcrumbs. Stir in the sugar. Add sufficient beaten egg to mix to a pliable dough.

Roll out the dough and use to line 4 individual Yorkshire pudding tins or tartlet tins (about 11 cm/4½ inches in diameter). Crimp the edges and prick the bottoms. Line with greaseproof paper weighed down with dried beans, then bake blind in a preheated oven for 15 minutes. Remove the paper and beans and bake for a further 5 minutes or until set and golden brown. Cool on a wire rack.

Cream the cheese with the lemon rind and sugar until smooth, then beat in sufficient lemon juice to give a spreading consistency. Spread over the bottom of the pastry cases and arrange the strawberries on top.

Dissolve the redcurrant jelly in the water, heating gently until liquid. Brush carefully over the strawberries. Chill before serving.

Variations:

Raspberries or grapes may be used in place of strawberries, with an appropriate glaze.

Summer pudding with rhubarb

Metric	Imperial
6–8 slices white bread, crusts removed	6–8 slices white bread, crusts removed
1 × 540 g can rhubarb	1 × 1 lb 3 oz can rhubarb
225 g blackcurrants	8 oz blackcurrants
225 g cooking apples, peeled, cored and sliced	8 oz cooking apples, peeled, cored and sliced
175 g sugar	6 oz sugar
100 g raspberries or strawberries	4 oz raspberries or strawberries

Preparation time: 20 minutes, plus chilling time
Cooking time: 5–10 minutes

Frozen fruit may be used for this recipe so that it can be made out of season. The secret to success in making summer pudding is to ensure that the slices of bread sit closely together, to make a firm case.

Put one slice of bread aside for the top and use the remainder to line the bottom and sides of a 1 litre/2 pint pudding basin, fitting the slices of bread closely together.

Drain the rhubarb, reserving 4 × 15 ml spoons/4 tablespoons of the can juice. Put the juice in a pan with the blackcurrants, apples and sugar and cook gently until tender but not too mushy, stirring occasionally. Add the raspberries or strawberries and continue cooking for 2 minutes. Spoon all the fruit into the bread-lined basin reserving a little of the juice, and cover with the last piece of bread. Fold the edges of the bread over the slice on top. Spoon the reserved juice down the sides of basin if necessary so that all the bread is coloured with the juice. Cover with a saucer and a weight or heavy can. Leave to cool, then chill thoroughly, preferably overnight or longer.

Turn out the pudding carefully just before serving it, with or without cream.

Summer pudding with rhubarb, Strawberry tartlets

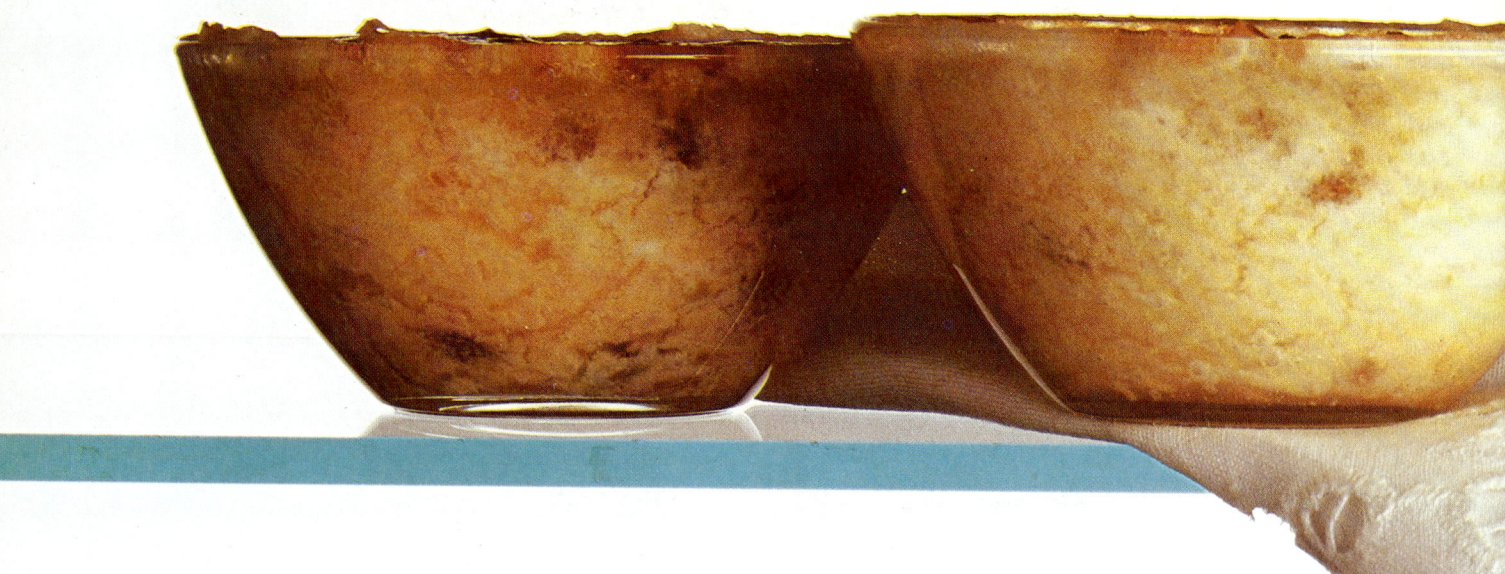

Apricot and lemon dreams

Metric
1 × 425 g can apricot
  halves
2 × 5 ml spoons powdered
  gelatine
grated rind of ½ lemon
2 × 15 ml spoons lemon
  juice
1 small can condensed
  milk
little whipped cream
  (optional)
coarsely grated chocolate
  or chopped toasted nuts,
  to decorate

Imperial
1 × 15 oz can apricot
  halves
2 teaspoons powdered
  gelatine
grated rind of ½ lemon
2 tablespoons lemon
  juice
1 small can condensed
  milk
little whipped cream
  (optional)
coarsely grated chocolate
  or chopped toasted nuts,
  to decorate

Preparation time: 10 minutes, plus about 20 minutes setting time

Remove 2 × 15 ml spoons/2 tablespoons of the apricot syrup from the can to a heatproof basin, mix in the gelatine and dissolve over a pan of hot water. Liquidize or sieve the apricots with the remaining syrup, then mix the purée with the lemon rind and juice, followed by the condensed milk. Stir the dissolved gelatine evenly through the mixture and pour into four glasses. Chill until set.
Decorate with a whirl of whipped cream and grated chocolate or nuts, or simply sprinkle with the chocolate or nuts.

Chocolate pear trifle

Metric
1 chocolate Swiss roll
1 × 425 g can pears
2 × 15 ml spoons rum
  (optional)
1 × 425 g can custard
40 g walnuts, chopped
few glacé cherries, to
  decorate

Imperial
1 chocolate Swiss roll
1 × 15 oz can pears
2 tablespoons rum
  (optional)
1 × 15 oz can custard
1½ oz walnuts, chopped
few glacé cherries, to
  decorate

Preparation time: 10 minutes

Cut the Swiss roll into slices and arrange half in a glass bowl. Drain the pears, reserving the syrup, and slice them. Arrange a layer of pear slices over the cake, reserving a few for decoration, then cover with the remaining Swiss roll slices.
Mix about 4 × 15 ml spoons/4 tablespoons of the pear syrup with the rum, if used, and spoon over the cake. Stir the custard until smooth and then pour evenly over the top.
Decorate with the remaining pear slices, sprinkle over the nuts and decorate with a few halved glacé cherries.

Rice and banana brûlée, Apricot and lemon dreams, Chocolate pear trifle

Rice and banana brûlée

10

Metric
1 × 425 g can creamed
  rice
2 bananas, sliced
50 g sultanas or seedless
  raisins (optional)
grated rind of ½ lemon
about 100 g caster sugar

Imperial
1 × 15 oz can creamed
  rice
2 bananas, sliced
2 oz sultanas or seedless
  raisins (optional)
grated rind of ½ lemon
about 4 oz caster sugar

Preparation time: 5 minutes
Cooking time: 5 minutes

Turn the creamed rice into a bowl and fold in the bananas, sultanas or raisins and lemon rind. Spoon into an ovenproof dish or four individual ramekin dishes and level the tops. Sprinkle a thick layer of caster sugar over the rice so that no rice is showing at all. Cook under a preheated hot grill until the sugar melts and turns brown to give a caramelized top. Serve hot or cold, tapping the caramel with a spoon to break it.

Profiteroles

Metric
50 g butter
150 ml water
65 g plain flour
pinch of salt
2 eggs, beaten

Chocolate sauce:
100 g plain chocolate
1 × 175 g can evaporated
    milk
few drops of vanilla
    essence

or Mocha sauce:
100 g plain chocolate
$\frac{3}{4}$ × 175 g can evaporated
    milk
2 × 15 ml spoons coffee
    essence

300 ml whipping cream
sifted icing sugar

Imperial
2 oz butter
$\frac{1}{4}$ pint water
$2\frac{1}{2}$ oz plain flour
pinch of salt
2 eggs, beaten

Chocolate sauce:
4 oz plain chocolate
1 × 6 oz can evaporated
    milk
few drops of vanilla
    essence

or Mocha sauce:
4 oz plain chocolate
$\frac{3}{4}$ × 6 oz can evaporated
    milk
2 tablespoons coffee
    essence

$\frac{1}{2}$ pint whipping cream
sifted icing sugar

Preparation time: 15 minutes
Cooking time: about 25 minutes
Oven: 220°C, 425°F, Gas Mark 7

To make a choux paste melt the butter in the water in a saucepan and bring to the boil. Sift the flour and salt together and add to the pan all at once. Beat until the mixture forms a smooth paste which leaves the sides of the pan clean. Remove from the heat and leave to cool slightly. Adding a little at a time gradually beat in the eggs until the mixture becomes glossy; incorporating as much air as possible. (The mixture must be firm enough to hold its shape.)
Put the choux paste into a piping bag fitted with a plain 2 cm/$\frac{3}{4}$ inch nozzle. Pipe out bun shapes about the size of a walnut on greased baking sheets, keeping the buns fairly well apart. Cook in a preheated oven for about 20 minutes or until well risen, golden brown and firm. Make a small hole in each bun to allow steam to escape and return to the oven for a few minutes to let the pastry dry out. Cool on a wire rack.
To make the chocolate or mocha sauce melt the chocolate in a heatproof basin over a pan of hot water. Gradually beat in the evaporated milk and essence until smooth. Keep the sauce warm.
Whip the cream until thick. Either split each profiterole in half and fill with cream, or using a piping bag fitted with a 5 mm/$\frac{1}{4}$ inch plain nozzle, make a small hole in the side of each profiterole and pipe in the cream. Pile the filled profiteroles in a pyramid and dredge with icing sugar. Serve the sauce separately.

Rich vanilla ice cream

Metric
300 ml double cream
3 × 15 ml spoons milk
75 g icing sugar, sifted
1 × 2.5 ml spoon vanilla
    essence
1 egg white

Imperial
$\frac{1}{2}$ pint double cream
3 tablespoons milk
3 oz icing sugar, sifted
$\frac{1}{2}$ teaspoon vanilla
    essence
1 egg white

Preparation time: about 10 minutes, plus freezing time

Set the refrigerator to the coldest setting 1 hour before you begin, unless you are using a freezer. Put the cream and milk into a bowl and whip until thick and standing in soft peaks; do not whip too stiffly. Fold in the icing sugar and vanilla essence and put into an ice-cube tray or basin. Freeze until the mixture is just firm but not hard.
Turn into a cold bowl, break down with a fork and beat until smooth. Whisk the egg white until very stiff and fold through the ice cream. Return to the ice-cube tray or basin and freeze until hard.
Serve with wafers and raspberries or other fruit.

Variations:
Orange or lemon: Stir in the finely grated rind of 1 orange or lemon after the first freezing.
Tutti frutti: Stir in 25 g/1 oz chopped toasted almonds, 40 g/$1\frac{1}{2}$ oz chopped glacé cherries, 40 g/$1\frac{1}{2}$ oz currants or sultanas and a little grated fruit rind after the first freezing.
Liqueur or coffee: Add 1–2 × 15 ml spoons/1–2 tablespoons liqueur or coffee essence to the basic mixture in place of the vanilla.
Ginger or nutty: Stir in 40 g/$1\frac{1}{2}$ oz very finely chopped preserved or stem ginger, or walnuts, almonds or hazelnuts after the first freezing.
Chocolate: Dissolve 2 × 15 ml spoons/2 tablespoons sifted cocoa powder in 3 × 15 ml spoons/3 tablespoons boiling water and leave until cold. Add after the first freezing.
Chocolate flake: Stir in 50 g/2 oz plain or milk chocolate, grated, after the first freezing.
Syllabub: Use 4 × 15 ml spoons/4 tablespoons white wine in place of the milk, omit the vanilla and add 1 × 5 ml spoon/1 teaspoon finely grated lemon rind after the first freezing.
Fruit: Fold 150 ml/$\frac{1}{4}$ pint thick fruit purée (e.g. raspberry, strawberry, blackberry, apricot etc.) into the whipped cream before freezing.

Profiteroles, Chocolate ice cream,
Chocolate flake ice cream, Rich vanilla ice cream

Coffee caramel cream

Metric	Imperial
2 eggs, separated	2 eggs, separated
50 g caster sugar	2 oz caster sugar
200 ml lukewarm milk	8 fl oz lukewarm milk
1 × 15 ml spoon coffee essence	1 tablespoon coffee essence
1 × 15 ml spoon Tia Maria or brandy (optional)	1 tablespoon Tia Maria or brandy (optional)
1 × 15 ml spoon powdered gelatine	1 tablespoon powdered gelatine
2 × 15 ml spoons water	2 tablespoons water
150 ml double cream	¼ pint double cream
50 g butter	2 oz butter
100 g digestive biscuits, crushed	4 oz digestive biscuits, crushed

Caramel:	Caramel:
75 g caster sugar	3 oz caster sugar
3 × 15 ml spoons water	3 tablespoons water

Preparation time: about 20 minutes, plus chilling time

Cream the egg yolks with the sugar until light and fluffy, then beat in the milk. Transfer to the top of a heatproof basin over a pan of gently simmering water and cook gently, stirring, until the custard thickens. Remove from the heat and stir in the coffee essence and Tia Maria or brandy.

Dissolve the gelatine in the water in a heatproof basin over a pan of hot water and stir into the coffee custard. Leave until the mixture is the consistency of unbeaten egg white.

Whip 90 ml/3 fl oz of the cream until thick. Whisk the egg whites until stiff. Fold first the whipped cream and then the egg whites into the custard and pour into a greased 900 ml/1½ pint ring mould. Chill until set. Melt the butter in a pan and stir in the biscuit crumbs. Spoon the crumb mixture in an even layer over the set mousse, pressing lightly until level. Chill until set. To make the caramel, dissolve the sugar in the water in a heavy-based pan, then bring to the boil. Boil hard until the mixture is caramel coloured. Pour quickly on to a greased baking sheet and leave to cool. When set, crush the caramel roughly with a rolling pin.

To serve, carefully unmould the coffee cream on to a plate, dipping it in hot water briefly if necessary to loosen. Whip the remaining cream until stiff and use to decorate the top of the ring and sprinkle with the crushed caramel.

Pineapple and apple flan

Metric	Imperial
125 g plain flour	5 oz plain flour
25 g custard powder	1 oz custard powder
2 × 5 ml spoons caster sugar	2 teaspoons caster sugar
75 g butter or margarine	3 oz butter or margarine
about 2 × 15 ml spoons milk	about 2 tablespoons milk

Filling:	Filling:
350–450 g cooking apples	12 oz–1 lb cooking apples
2 × 15 ml spoons sugar (optional)	2 tablespoons sugar (optional)
1 × 375 g can crushed pineapple, drained	1 × 13 oz can crushed pineapple, drained
grated rind of ½ lemon	grated rind of ½ lemon
3 × 15 ml spoons clear honey	3 tablespoons clear honey

milk, to glaze   milk, to glaze

Preparation time: 10 minutes
Cooking time: about 35 minutes
Oven: 190°C, 375°F, Gas Mark 5

To make the pastry, sift the flour and custard powder into a bowl and mix in the sugar. Rub in the fat until the mixture resembles fine breadcrumbs, then add sufficient milk to mix to a pliable dough. Break off about one-quarter of the dough and set aside. Roll out the remaining dough and use to line a 20 cm/8 inch flan ring or tin.

Peel, core and very thinly slice the apples. Lay them in the pastry case and sprinkle with the sugar. Combine the pineapple, lemon rind and 2½ × 15 ml spoons/2½ tablespoons of the honey and spread over the apple.

Roll out the reserved dough and cut into 5 mm/¼ inch wide strips. Lay these over the filling in a lattice design. Dampen the ends and press to seal to the pastry case. Brush the strips with milk and bake in a preheated oven for about 35 minutes or until the pastry is golden brown. Brush the pastry lattice with the remaining honey and serve hot or cold, with cream or ice cream.

Coffee caramel cream, Pineapple and apple flan, Peach cream flan

Peach cream flan

Preparation time: 10 minutes
Cooking time: about 20 minutes
Oven: 200°C, 400°F, Gas Mark 6

Metric
100 g plain flour
50 g butter or margarine
15 g lard
2 × 5 ml spoons caster
   sugar
1 egg yolk
cold water (optional)

Imperial
4 oz plain flour
2 oz butter or margarine
½ oz lard
2 teaspoons caster
   sugar
1 egg yolk
cold water (optional)

Filling:
200 ml milk
50–65 g caster sugar
1½ × 15 ml spoons
   cornflour
few drops of almond
   essence
2 egg yolks
1 × 425 g can peach
   slices, drained

Filling:
8 fl oz milk
2–2½ oz caster sugar
1½ tablespoons
   cornflour
few drops of almond
   essence
2 egg yolks
1 × 15 oz can peach
   slices, drained

To decorate:
whipping cream
pistachio nuts or strips
   of candied angelica

To decorate:
whipping cream
pistachio nuts or strips
   of candied angelica

Sift the flour into a bowl and rub in the fats until the mixture resembles breadcrumbs. Mix together the sugar and egg yolk and add to the flour mixture with a little cold water if necessary to mix to a pliable dough. Roll out the dough and use to line a 20 cm/8 inch flan ring or dish. Line with greaseproof paper weighed down with dried beans and bake blind in a preheated oven for 15 minutes. Remove the beans and paper and bake for a further 5 minutes or until set and golden brown. Cool on a wire rack.

To make the filling, put the milk, sugar and cornflour in a small saucepan and bring to the boil, stirring continuously. Boil for 1 minute, then beat in the almond essence and egg yolks. Cook gently for a further minute, then pour into the flan case and leave to cool. Arrange the peach slices over the custard filling. Decorate around the peaches with stars of whipped cream and top with chopped pistachio nuts or pieces of angelica.

Variation:
Other canned fruit or fresh soft fruit may be used in place of peaches.

85

Mincemeat meringue pie

Metric	*Imperial*
100 g plain flour	*4 oz plain flour*
pinch of salt	*pinch of salt*
65 g hard margarine	*2½ oz hard margarine*
1 × 15 ml spoon caster sugar	*1 tablespoon caster sugar*
about 1 × 15 ml spoon milk	*about 1 tablespoon milk*
225–350 g mincemeat	*8–12 oz mincemeat*
grated rind of 1 lemon	*grated rind of 1 lemon*
2 egg whites	*2 egg whites*
100 g caster sugar	*4 oz caster sugar*

Preparation time: 10 minutes
Cooking time: about 45 minutes
Oven: 200°C, 400°F, Gas Mark 6
　　　　160°C, 325°F, Gas Mark 3

To make the pastry, sift the flour and salt into a bowl and rub in the fat until the mixture resembles bread-crumbs. Stir in the sugar, then add sufficient milk to bind to a pliable dough. Roll out carefully on a floured surface and use to line a deep 20 cm/8 inch pie dish or tin, crimping the edges.

Mix together the mincemeat and lemon rind and spread evenly in the pastry case. Bake in a preheated oven for about 25 minutes or until the pastry is lightly browned and cooked through. Remove the pie and reduce the oven temperature.

Whisk the egg whites until they are very stiff, then gradually whisk in the sugar, making sure the meringue becomes stiff again after each addition of sugar. Put into a piping bag fitted with a star vegetable nozzle. Pipe a lattice design over the mincemeat and a circle of stars around the edge. Return the pie to the oven and bake for 15–20 minutes or until the meringue is lightly tinged brown. Serve hot or cold.

Puff-topped fruit pie

Preparation time: about 20 minutes
Cooking time: about 50 minutes
Oven: 220°C, 425°F, Gas Mark 7
    190°C, 375°F, Gas Mark 5

Metric
100 g plain flour
pinch of salt
25 g butter or margarine
25 g lard
about 1 × 15 ml spoon
   water

Imperial
4 oz plain flour
pinch of salt
1 oz butter or margarine
1 oz lard
about 1 tablespoon
   water

Rough puff pastry:
100 g plain flour
pinch of salt
75 g hard margarine,
   chilled
about 4 × 15 ml spoons
   iced water

Rough puff pastry:
4 oz plain flour
pinch of salt
3 oz hard margarine,
   chilled
about 4 tablespoons
   iced water

Filling:
750 g cooking apples,
   peeled, cored and sliced
about 100 g sugar
grated rind of ½ lemon
   or orange

milk or beaten egg, to
   glaze
sugar for dredging
   (optional)

Filling:
1½ lb cooking apples,
   peeled, cored and sliced
about 4 oz sugar
grated rind of ½ lemon
   or orange

milk or beaten, to
   glaze
sugar for dredging
   (optional)

To make the shortcrust pastry, sift 100 g/4 oz plain flour and a pinch of salt into a bowl and rub in 25 g/1 oz each of butter and lard until the mixture resembles breadcrumbs. Add sufficient water to mix to a pliable dough. Wrap in polythene and chill.

Meanwhile make the rough puff pastry. Sift the flour and salt into a bowl. Coarsely grate the chilled margarine into the flour and mix well. Add sufficient water to mix to a firm dough. On a floured surface roll out the dough to a narrow strip, and fold the bottom third up and the top third down. Seal the edges by pressing with a rolling pin, then give the dough a quarter turn so the folds are at the side. Repeat the rolling out and folding twice more, then wrap in polythene and chill. To make the filling mix the apples with the sugar and fruit rind. Roll out the shortcrust pastry and use to line a 22 cm/8½ inch pie dish or tin that is about 4 cm/1½ inches deep. Pack in the apples tightly. Roll out the rough puff pastry for the lid. Dampen the edges and place the lid in position. Press the edges well together to seal and trim off any surplus dough. Flake the edge and scallop with the back of a knife, then decorate the top of the pie with the dough trimmings. Make a hole in the centre and brush all over with milk or beaten egg.

Bake in a preheated oven for 25–30 minutes or until lightly browned, then reduce the oven temperature and continue baking for 15–20 minutes. Serve hot, sprinkled with sugar, and with cream, custard or vanilla ice cream.

Variations:
Use gooseberries, rhubarb, plums, apricots, blackcurrants, or a mixture of apple and another fruit.

Puff-topped fruit pie, Mincemeat meringue pie

Cherry kissel

Metric	Imperial
300 ml red or white wine	$\frac{1}{2}$ pint red or white wine
450 ml water	$\frac{3}{4}$ pint water
100 g caster sugar	4 oz caster sugar
450 g cherries, stoned	1 lb cherries, stoned
2 × 15 ml spoons arrowroot	2 tablespoons arrowroot
2–3 × 15 ml spoons Kirsch or cherry brandy (optional)	2–3 tablespoons Kirsch or cherry brandy (optional)

Preparation time: about 10 minutes
Cooking time: 30 minutes

Put the wine and 300 ml/$\frac{1}{2}$ pint water in a pan with the sugar. Heat gently until the sugar has dissolved, then add the cherries. Bring slowly to the boil, then lower the heat and simmer for about 15 minutes until the cherries are soft but still whole.
Strain the liquid through a sieve, then put the cherries in individual glass serving bowls. Return the liquid to the rinsed-out pan and heat gently.
Mix the remaining water to a paste with the arrowroot, then stir gradually into the liquid in the pan. Bring to the boil, then lower the heat and simmer for 1 to 2 minutes until thick and clear, stirring constantly with a wooden spoon. Stir in the Kirsch or brandy, then pour over the cherries in the bowls. Serve warm or chilled, with sweetened whipped cream or soured cream.

Caramel bananas

Metric	Imperial
50 g unsalted butter	2 oz unsalted butter
4 × 15 ml spoons dark soft brown sugar	4 tablespoons dark soft brown sugar
150 ml water	$\frac{1}{4}$ pint water
grated rind of 1 orange	grated rind of 1 orange
juice of 2 oranges	juice of 2 oranges
1 × 1.25 ml spoon ground cinnamon	$\frac{1}{4}$ teaspoon ground cinnamon
4 bananas	4 bananas

Preparation time: 10 minutes
Cooking time: 15 minutes

Melt the butter in a large heavy frying pan. Add the sugar and heat gently until dissolved, stirring constantly. Add the remaining ingredients, except the bananas, then bring to the boil, stirring all the time.
Peel the bananas and cut in half lengthways. Arrange the bananas in a single layer in the pan, lower the heat and simmer for about 10 minutes until the bananas are tender. Spoon the sauce over the bananas during cooking. Serve hot with cream.

Apricot rice condé

Metric	Imperial
100 g short-grain rice	4 oz short-grain rice
600 ml milk	1 pint milk
1 vanilla pod	1 vanilla pod
100 g caster sugar	4 oz caster sugar
25 g unsalted butter	1 oz unsalted butter
4 egg yolks, lightly beaten	4 egg yolks, lightly beaten
150 ml whipping or double cream	$\frac{1}{4}$ pint whipping or double cream
1 × 15 ml spoon powdered gelatine	1 tablespoon powdered gelatine
4 × 15 ml spoons sherry, dry white wine or water	4 tablespoons sherry, dry white wine or water
150 ml water	$\frac{1}{4}$ pint water
350 g fresh apricots, halved and stoned, with 100 g caster sugar and 150 ml water, or 1 × 400 g can apricots	12 oz fresh apricots, halved and stoned, with 4 oz caster sugar and $\frac{1}{4}$ pint water, or 1 × 15 g can apricots

Preparation time: 50 minutes, plus chilling time
Cooking time: 1 hour 25 minutes

Put the rice and milk in a pan and bring to the boil. Lower the heat, then add the vanilla pod, 50 g/2 oz of the caster sugar and the butter. Stirring frequently simmer, uncovered, for 30 minutes until the rice is tender and has absorbed all the milk.
Meanwhile, put the egg yolks and the remaining caster sugar in a heatproof bowl and stir well. Put the cream in a heavy pan and bring slowly to just below boiling point, then stir into the egg yolk mixture. Stand the bowl in a pan of hot water and heat gently until the custard thickens, stirring constantly.
Sprinkle the gelatine over the sherry in a small heatproof bowl, then leave until spongy. Stand the bowl in a pan of hot water and heat gently until the gelatine has dissolved, stirring occasionally. Stir slowly into the egg custard. When the rice is cooked, remove the vanilla pod and stir in the custard mixture.
Pour the mixture into a lightly oiled 15 cm/6 inch soufflé dish, then chill overnight until set.
If using fresh apricots, put 100 g/4 oz caster sugar in a pan with the water and heat gently until the sugar has dissolved. Add the apricot halves and poach gently for about 10 minutes until just tender. Remove from the pan with a perforated spoon and cool. Meanwhile, boil the liquid until syrupy, then cool. Loosen the edge of the rice condé with a sharp knife, then turn out on to a serving dish. Just before serving, arrange the fresh or canned apricots on top and around the condé, spoon over the syrup and if liked sprinkle with toasted almonds. Serve chilled.

Caramel bananas, Apricot rice condé, Cherry kissel

Marzipan fritters, Toffee apples, Ginger beer apple fritters

Marzipan fritters

25

Metric	*Imperial*
225 g marzipan (in a block)	8 oz marzipan (in a block)
100 g plain flour	4 oz plain flour
pinch of salt	pinch of salt
1 egg	1 egg
150 ml milk	¼ pint milk
oil or fat for deep frying	oil or fat for deep frying
caster sugar	caster sugar

Preparation time: 20 minutes
Cooking time: about 5 minutes

Cut the marzipan into about 16 fingers 1 cm/½ inch wide. Sift the flour and salt into a bowl. Add the egg and gradually beat in the milk. Start heating the oil or fat in a large pan for deep frying.
Dip each finger of marzipan into the batter until evenly coated. Lower the marzipan fingers into the hot fat and fry for 3 to 4 minutes until crisp and golden. Drain well on kitchen paper and serve hot, sprinkled with caster sugar.

Toffee apples

30

Metric	*Imperial*
4 eating apples	4 eating apples
juice of 1 lemon	juice of 1 lemon
200 ml water	⅓ pint water
225 g granulated sugar	8 oz granulated sugar
75 g butter	3 oz butter
pinch of mixed spice	pinch of mixed spice

Preparation time: 15 minutes
Cooking time: about 15 minutes

Peel and core the apples. Cut the apples into rings 5 mm/¼ inch thick. Toss the apple rings in lemon juice to prevent discolouration.
Put the water and sugar into a pan. Stir over a gentle heat until the sugar has dissolved. Increase the heat and boil gently, without stirring, until a golden syrup. Meanwhile, drain the apple rings. Heat the butter in a large shallow pan. Add the apple rings and fry until lightly golden on both sides. Sprinkle with spice. Transfer the apple slices to a serving dish and spoon over the toffee sauce. Serve hot with cream.

Ginger beer apple fritters

Metric
100 g plain flour
pinch of salt
1 egg, separated
1 × 15 ml spoon oil
150 ml ginger beer
50 g caster sugar
3 medium cooking apples
oil or fat for deep frying
demerara or caster sugar
  and orange wedges, to
  serve

Imperial
4 oz plain flour
pinch of salt
1 egg, separated
1 tablespoon oil
¼ pint ginger beer
2 oz caster sugar
3 medium cooking apples
oil or fat for deep frying
demerara or caster sugar
  and orange wedges, to
  serve

Preparation time: 15 minutes
Cooking time: about 15 minutes

On occasions when you have more time, the batter is even better if made in advance – make it as below, without the egg white, then cover and store in a cool place. Fold in the beaten egg white just before using. Sift the flour and salt into a bowl. Add the egg yolk and the spoonful of oil, and gradually beat in the ginger beer. Stir in the caster sugar. Start heating the oil or fat for deep frying whilst preparing the apples.

Peel and core the apples and cut into 5 mm/¼ inch thick rings. Put the apple rings into a bowl of salted water to prevent discolouration.

Beat the egg white until stiff and fold it into the batter. Drain the apple rings well on kitchen paper, then dip each ring into the ginger beer batter and then lower it into the hot fat. Fry about 4 fritters at a time until crisp and golden on both sides. Drain well and serve hot, sprinkled with sugar, and accompanied by wedges of orange.

Traditional Teatime

Sunday afternoon tea is not quite the same as it used to be, but many of the favourites of that rather special teatable linger on. All the family will enjoy home-made bread, from the time the smell of the loaves fresh from the oven permeates the house until the last crumb is finished, and home-made scones served still warm will disappear very quickly. Children love biscuits and cookies; other members of the family may prefer an elegant cream slice or a piece of moist coffee cake. Whatever it is, something will tempt everyone.

Cranberry teabread

Metric	Imperial
100 g fresh or frozen cranberries	*4 oz fresh or frozen cranberries*
2 × 15 ml spoons orange juice	*2 tablespoons orange juice*
6 × 15 ml spoons water	*6 tablespoons water*
25 g butter or margarine	*1 oz butter or margarine*
175 g caster or soft brown sugar	*6 oz caster or soft brown sugar*
300 g self-raising flour	*10 oz self-raising flour*
pinch of salt	*pinch of salt*
grated rind of 1 orange	*grated rind of 1 orange*
50 g walnuts, chopped	*2 oz walnuts, chopped*
1 egg, beaten	*1 egg, beaten*

Preparation time: 15 minutes
Cooking time: about 50 minutes
Oven: 180 °C, 350°F, Gas Mark 4

Put the cranberries, orange juice, water, butter or margarine and sugar into a small pan and bring slowly to the boil, stirring until the sugar has dissolved. Simmer for 5 minutes, then remove from the heat and leave to cool.
Sift the flour and salt into a bowl and mix in the orange rind and nuts. Add the egg and cranberry mixture and beat well. Place in a greased and lined 900 g/2 lb loaf tin and smooth the top.
Bake in a preheated oven for about 50 minutes or until well risen and firm to the touch. Turn on to a wire rack to cool. Serve in slices, plain or buttered.

Variation:
For an apricot tealoaf, replace the cranberries with chopped dried apricots.

Mini Bakewell tarts, Cranberry teabread

Mini Bakewell tarts

Metric	Imperial
100 g plain flour	*4 oz plain flour*
pinch of salt	*pinch of salt*
25 g butter or margarine	*1 oz butter or margarine*
25 g lard	*1 oz lard*
cold water, to mix	*cold water, to mix*

Filling:	*Filling:*
50 g butter or margarine	*2 oz butter or margarine*
50 g caster or light soft brown sugar	*2 oz caster or light soft brown sugar*
1 egg (sizes 1, 2), beaten	*1 egg (sizes 1, 2), beaten*
few drops of almond essence	*few drops of almond essence*
40 g self-raising flour	*1½ oz self-raising flour*
25 g ground almonds	*1 oz ground almonds*
raspberry jam	*raspberry jam*
icing sugar for dredging	*icing sugar for dredging*

Preparation time: 20 minutes
Cooking time: 15–20 minutes
Oven: 200°C, 400°F, Gas Mark 6

To make the pastry, sift the flour and salt into a bowl and rub in the fats until the mixture resembles fine breadcrumbs. Add sufficient water to mix to a pliable dough, then knead lightly. Roll out thinly on a lightly floured surface. Cut into about 16 circles using a 7.5 cm/3 inch plain or fluted cutter and use to line dampened or lightly greased patty tins.
To make the filling, cream together the butter or margarine and sugar until very light and fluffy, then beat in the egg and a few drops of almond essence. Beat in the flour and finally fold in the ground almonds. Spread a little raspberry jam in the bottom of each pastry case and cover with the filling so each tart is about half full. Bake in a preheated hot oven for 15–20 minutes or until well risen and golden brown. Cool on a wire rack, then dredge with icing sugar.
Makes about 16

Variation:
A thin layer of Glacé Icing (page 106) may be spread on top of each tart in place of the icing sugar.

Oatmeal plait

Metric	Imperial
400 g strong plain white flour	14 oz strong plain white flour
1 × 5 ml spoon salt	1 teaspoon salt
1 × 5 ml spoon caster sugar	1 teaspoon caster sugar
25 g lard	1 oz lard
100 g oatmeal (fine or medium)	4 oz oatmeal (fine or medium)
15 g fresh yeast, or 1½ × 5 ml spoons dried yeast and 1 × 5 ml spoon caster sugar	½ oz fresh yeast, or 1½ teaspoons dried yeast and 1 teaspoon caster sugar
150 ml warm milk (43°C)	¼ pint warm milk (110°F)
150 ml warm water (43°C)	¼ pint warm water (110°F)
milk or water, to glaze	milk or water, to glaze
little coarse oatmeal	little coarse oatmeal

Preparation time: 25 minutes, plus rising time
Cooking time: 30–35 minutes
Oven: 230°C, 450°F, Gas Mark 8

This dough may be used to make two smaller plaits or a cob loaf, or 10–12 rolls. Smaller plaits take 20–25 minutes baking and rolls 15–20 minutes.

Sift the flour, salt and sugar into a bowl, rub in the lard, then mix in the oatmeal. If using fresh yeast dissolve it in the milk and water; or for dried yeast dissolve the sugar in the liquid and sprinkle the yeast on top. Leave in a warm place for about 10 minutes or until frothy. Add the yeast liquid to the dry ingredients and mix to form a fairly soft dough. Turn out on to a floured surface and knead for 10 minutes or until smooth and no longer sticky (or for 3–4 minutes in an electric mixer fitted with a dough hook). Shape the dough into a ball, place in an oiled polythene bag and tie loosely at the top. Put to rise in a warm place for about 1 hour or until doubled in size.
Remove the dough from the bag, knock back and knead for about 2 minutes or until smooth. Divide into three equal pieces. Roll into three sausage shapes, which are all the same length and about 4 cm/1½ inches in diameter. Lay the lengths close to each other and beginning in the middle, plait towards you. Pinch the ends together to secure them. Turn the plait round and complete the plait, again securing the ends. Place on a greased baking sheet, brush with milk or water and sprinkle with coarse oatmeal. Cover with a sheet of oiled polythene and leave to rise in a warm place until doubled in size.
Bake in a preheated oven for 25–35 minutes or until well risen and lightly browned and the plait sounds hollow when the base is tapped. Cool on a wire rack.

Floury scones

Metric	Imperial
200 g self-raising flour	8 oz self-raising flour
pinch of salt	pinch of salt
50 g butter or margarine	2 oz butter or margarine
25 g caster sugar	1 oz caster sugar
40 g sultanas (optional)	1½ oz sultanas (optional)
1 egg, beaten	1 egg, beaten
4–5 × 5 ml spoons milk (preferably soured)	4–5 tablespoons milk (preferably soured)
flour for dredging	flour for dredging

Preparation time: 5 minutes
Cooking time: 12–15 minutes
Oven: 230°C, 450°F, Gas Mark 8

To make a scone round, shape all the dough into a flattish round about 18 cm/7 inches across and place on the baking sheet. Mark deeply into 8 or 10 wedges and bake for 15–20 minutes.

Sift the flour and salt into a bowl and rub in the fat until the mixture resembles fine breadcrumbs. Stir in the sugar and sultanas, then bind to a fairly soft dough with the egg and milk.
Turn on to a floured surface, knead lightly and flatten out to about 2–2.5 cm/¾–1 inch thick with the palm of your hand. Cut into triangles, squares or 5 cm/2 inch rounds and dredge fairly thickly with flour. Place on well-floured or greased baking sheets.
Bake in a preheated oven for 12–15 minutes or until well risen, lightly browned and firm to the touch. Turn on to a wire rack covered with a clean cloth, wrap and leave to cool. Serve fresh, split, buttered and with jam or honey.
Makes 10

Variations:
Lemon and date scones: Add the finely grated rind of 1 lemon and 40 g/1½ oz, finely chopped, stoned dates, in place of the sultanas.
Spiced scones: Replace the sultanas with 25 g/1 oz each of currants and chopped mixed peel. Add 1 × 5 ml spoon/1 teaspoon mixed spice to the dry ingredients.
Honey walnut scones: Replace the sultanas with 25–40 g/1–1½ oz chopped walnuts, and 1 × 15 ml spoon/1 tablespoon of the milk with clear honey.
Savoury scones: Omit the sugar and sultanas and add either 50 g/2 oz mature Cheddar cheese grated; or 2 × 15 ml spoons/2 tablespoons grated Parmesan cheese; or 1½ × 5 ml spoons/1½ teaspoons mixed dried herbs; or 40 g/1½ oz finely chopped salted peanuts; or 50 g/2 oz crisply fried bacon, finely chopped.
Wholemeal scones: Use 100 g/4 oz wholemeal flour and add 1 × 5 ml spoon/1 teaspoon baking powder.

Oatmeal plait, Floury scones

Quick brown bread

Metric	*Imperial*
225 g strong plain white flour	8 oz strong plain white flour
225 g wholemeal flour	8 oz wholemeal flour
$1\frac{1}{2}$ × 5 ml spoons salt	$1\frac{1}{2}$ teaspoons salt
2 × 5 ml spoons sugar	2 teaspoons sugar
15 g lard	$\frac{1}{2}$ oz lard
15 g fresh yeast, or 2 × 5 ml spoons dried yeast and 1 × 5 ml spoon caster sugar	$\frac{1}{2}$ oz fresh yeast, or 2 teaspoons dried yeast and 1 teaspoon caster sugar
300 ml warm water (43°C)	$\frac{1}{2}$ pint warm water (110°F)
salted water, to glaze	salted water, to glaze
cracked wheat or oatmeal	cracked wheat or oatmeal

Preparation time: 15 minutes, plus rising time
Cooking time: 30–40 minutes
Oven: 230°C, 450°F, Gas Mark 8
200°C, 400°F, Gas Mark 6

This bread does not keep fresh as long as loaves made with two risings, but it is very good when fresh and excellent toasted.

Sift the white flour into a bowl and mix in the wholemeal flour, salt and sugar. Rub in the lard. If using fresh yeast dissolve it in the warm water; or for dried yeast dissolve the sugar in the water and sprinkle the yeast on top. Leave in a warm place for about 10 minutes or until frothy.
Add the yeast liquid to the dry ingredients and mix to form a fairly firm dough. Turn on to a floured surface and knead for about 10 minutes or until smooth and no longer sticky. (Kneading in a large electric mixer fitted with a dough hook will take only 3–4 minutes.) Use all the dough, or divide the dough in half and shape either into one round ball, or a small baton by rolling backwards and forwards with the palms of the hands, or one of each. Place on greased baking sheets, brush the tops with salted water and sprinkle with cracked wheat or oatmeal. Cover lightly with oiled polythene and leave to rise in a warm place until doubled in size. Remove the polythene and bake in a preheated oven for 15 minutes, then reduce the temperature and continue baking for about 10 minutes for 2 small loaves or 20 minutes for one large one, or until the loaves sound hollow when the bases are tapped. Cool on a wire rack.
Makes 2 loaves

Quick brown bread, White bread, White bread rolls

White bread

Metric
700 g strong plain white
  flour
2 × 5 ml spoons salt
15 g lard
15 g fresh yeast, or
  1½ × 5 ml spoons dried
  yeast and 1 × 5 ml
  spoon caster sugar
450 ml warm water
  (43°C)
beaten egg or milk, to
  glaze (optional)
poppy seeds or sesame
  seeds (optional)

Imperial
1½ lb strong plain white
  flour
2 teaspoons salt
½ oz lard
½ oz fresh yeast, or
  1½ teaspoons dried
  yeast and 1 teaspoon
  caster sugar
¾ pint warm water
  (110°F)
beaten egg or milk, to
  glaze (optional)
poppy seeds or sesame
  seeds (optional)

Preparation time: 25 minutes, plus rising time
Cooking time: 30–40 minutes for loaves and 15–20 minutes for rolls
Oven: 230°C, 450°F, Gas Mark 8

Sift the flour and salt into a bowl and rub in the lard. If using fresh yeast dissolve it in the warm water; or for dried yeast dissolve the sugar in the water and sprinkle the yeast on top. Leave in a warm place for about 10 minutes or until frothy.

Add the yeast liquid to the dry ingredients and mix to form a firm elastic dough using a palette knife. Turn on to a lightly floured surface and knead for about 10 minutes or until smooth and no longer sticky. To do this punch the dough down and away from you using the palm of your hand then fold it over towards you, give a quarter turn and repeat.

The dough can also be mixed and kneaded in a large electric mixer fitted with a dough hook, following the manufacturer's instructions; this will take 3–4 minutes.

Shape the dough into a ball, place in a large oiled polythene bag and tie loosely at the top. Put to rise in a warm place for about 1 hour or until doubled in size and the dough springs back when lightly pressed with a floured finger.

Remove the dough from the bag, knock back and knead for about 2 minutes or until smooth again. Divide the dough into two portions – two-thirds and one-third. Shape into loaves and place in a greased 900 g/2 lb loaf tin and a 450 g/1 lb tin. For three small loaves divide the dough into three, shape into loaves and place in three 450 g/1 lb loaf tins. For rolls, divide the dough into 50 g/2 oz pieces and shape into small rounds or finger shapes with slightly tapering ends. Place on greased baking sheets, fairly close together for soft sided rolls but well apart for crisp ones. Cover lightly with oiled polythene and put to rise in a warm place until the dough reaches the tops of the tins or the rolls have doubled in size.

Before baking, the dough may be glazed with beaten egg or milk and sprinkled with poppy or sesame seeds. Alternatively, simply dredge with flour instead of glazing. Bake in a preheated oven allowing 35–40 minutes for a large loaf, about 30 minutes for smaller loaves and 15–20 minutes for rolls. When ready the loaves should be well risen and golden brown and sound hollow when the bases are tapped. Cool on a wire rack. Makes 1 large and 1 small or 3 small loaves, or about 15 rolls.

Variations:
Brown Bread: Make as above but use strong wholemeal flour and increase the yeast content to 25 g/1 oz fresh yeast or 1 × 15 ml spoon/1 tablespoon dried yeast.
  Light Brown Bread: Make as above but replace one-third to half the white flour with a strong wholemeal flour.

Iced gingerbread

Metric	Imperial
225 g plain flour	8 oz plain flour
1 × 5 ml spoon mixed spice	1 teaspoon mixed spice
2 × 5 ml spoons ground ginger	2 teaspoons ground ginger
1 × 5 ml spoon bicarbonate of soda	1 teaspoon bicarbonate of soda
100 g butter or margarine	4 oz butter or margarine
50 g dark soft brown sugar	2 oz dark soft brown sugar
50 g black treacle	2 oz black treacle
150 g golden syrup	6 oz golden syrup
2 eggs, beaten	2 eggs, beaten
150 ml milk	¼ pint milk

Lemon icing:

100 g icing sugar	4 oz icing sugar
1–2 × 15 ml spoons lemon juice	1–2 tablespoons lemon juice
yellow food colouring (optional)	yellow food colouring (optional)
lemon jelly slices or pieces of stem or crystallized ginger, to decorate	lemon jelly slices or pieces of stem or crystallized ginger, to decorate

Preparation time: 10 minutes
Cooking time: 1¼–1½ hours
Oven: 150°C, 300°F, Gas Mark 2

Sift the flour, spice, ginger and soda together. Melt the butter or margarine, sugar, treacle and syrup in a saucepan but do not overheat; cool until lukewarm. Add the melted mixture, eggs and milk to the dry ingredients and beat until smooth.

Pour into a greased and lined 18 cm/7 inch square cake tin and bake in a preheated oven for 1¼–1½ hours or until firm to the touch and a skewer inserted in the centre of the cake comes out clean. Cool in the tin, then turn out on to a wire rack.

To make the icing, sift the icing sugar into a bowl and beat in sufficient strained lemon juice and a few drops of colouring to give a thick spreading consistency. Spread over the top of the gingerbread. Just before the icing sets, decorate with lemon jelly slices or pieces of ginger.

Variation:

Plain white icing made with water instead of lemon juice and without food colouring may be used.

Grantham gingerbreads

Metric	Imperial
100 g butter or margarine	4 oz butter or margarine
300 g caster sugar	12 oz caster sugar
1 egg (sizes 1, 2), beaten	1 egg (sizes 1, 2), beaten
250 g self-raising flour	9 oz self-raising flour
1½–2 × 5 ml spoons ground ginger	1½–2 teaspoons ground ginger

Lemon Icing:

100 g icing sugar, sifted	4 oz icing sugar, sifted
lemon juice	lemon juice

Preparation time: 15 minutes
Cooking time: about 40 minutes
Oven: 150°C, 300°F, Gas Mark 2

When these irresistibly light biscuits are baked they should be hollow inside.

Cream the fat until soft, then gradually beat in the sugar and continue beating until well mixed. Add the egg followed by the flour sifted with the ginger and knead well to give a smooth and pliable dough. Divide the dough into pieces about the size of a walnut and roll into balls.

Place the balls fairly well apart on greased baking sheets and bake in a preheated oven for about 40 minutes or until well puffed up and lightly browned. Cool on a wire rack.

To make the icing, put the sugar into a bowl and add sufficient lemon juice to give a fairly soft consistency. Put into a greaseproof paper icing bag, cut off the tip and drizzle the icing over the biscuits. When set and cold store in an airtight container.

Makes about 25

Variation:

Use orange icing instead of lemon by substituting orange for lemon juice.

Iced gingerbread, Peanut cookies, Grantham gingerbreads

Peanut cookies

Preparation time: 15 minutes
Cooking time: about 25 minutes
Oven: 180°C, 350°F, Gas Mark 4

Metric	Imperial
50 g smooth peanut butter	*2 oz smooth peanut butter*
50 g butter or margarine, softened	*2 oz butter or margarine, softened*
grated rind of ½ lemon or orange	*grated rind of ½ lemon or orange*
50 g caster sugar	*2 oz caster sugar*
40 g light soft brown sugar	*1½ oz light soft brown sugar*
½ egg, beaten	*½ egg, beaten*
40 g seedless raisins or sultanas, chopped	*1½ oz seedless raisins or sultanas, chopped*
100 g self-raising flour	*4 oz self-raising flour*
25–40 g salted or unsalted peanuts, chopped	*1–1½ oz salted or unsalted peanuts, chopped*

Cream together the peanut butter and fat until soft, then add the fruit rind and sugars and continue creaming until light and fluffy. Beat in the egg followed by the dried fruit and flour and mix to a firm dough. Roll into balls about the size of a walnut and place fairly well apart on lightly greased baking sheets. Flatten each biscuit a little and mark a criss-cross pattern on top with a fork or round-bladed knife. Sprinkle each with a few of the chopped peanuts. Bake in a preheated oven for about 25 minutes or until well risen and golden brown. Cool on a wire rack, then store in an airtight container.
Makes about 18

Coffee fudge cake

Metric	Imperial
150 g butter or margarine	*6 oz butter or margarine*
150 g soft brown sugar	*6 oz soft brown sugar*
3 eggs	*3 eggs*
150 g self-raising flour, sifted	*6 oz self-raising flour, sifted*
1 × 15 ml spoon coffee essence or very strong black coffee	*1 tablespoon coffee essence or very strong black coffee*
1 × 15 ml spoon black treacle	*1 tablespoon black treacle*

Filling:	Filling:
100 g butter	*4 oz butter*
225 g icing sugar, sifted	*8 oz icing sugar, sifted*
1 × 15 ml spoon coffee essence or very strong black coffee	*1 tablespoon coffee essence or very strong black coffee*
1 × 15 ml spoon black treacle	*1 tablespoon black treacle*
orange and lemon jelly slices, almonds or toasted hazelnuts, to decorate	*orange and lemon jelly slices, almonds or toasted hazelnuts, to decorate*

Preparation time: 15 minutes
Cooking time: 20–25 minutes
Oven: 190°C, 375°F, Gas Mark 5

Grease and base line two 20 cm/8 inch deep sandwich tins and dredge with flour. Cream together the fat and sugar until very light and fluffy, and pale in colour. Beat in the eggs one at a time, following each with a spoonful of the flour. Using a metal spoon fold in the remaining flour alternately with the coffee and treacle.

Divide between the two tins, level the tops and bake in a preheated oven for about 20 minutes or until well risen and just firm to the touch. Turn out on to a wire rack and leave to cool.

To make the filling, cream the butter until soft, then gradually beat in the icing sugar alternating with the coffee and treacle to give a smooth spreading consistency. Use about one-third of the icing to sandwich the cakes together, then spread half of the remaining icing over the top of the cake and mark it into a pattern with a round-bladed knife. Put the rest of the icing into a piping bag fitted with a star nozzle and pipe horizontal lines of shells across the top of the cake. Decorate with orange and lemon slices, almonds or toasted hazelnuts.

Variation:

For a coffee cake simply leave out the black treacle in both the cake and icing.

Speedy chocolate cake

Metric	Imperial
175 g plain flour	*6 oz plain flour*
25 g cocoa powder	*1 oz cocoa powder*
1 × 5 ml spoon baking powder	*1 teaspoon baking powder*
1 × 5 ml spoon bicarbonate of soda	*1 teaspoon bicarbonate of soda*
125 g light soft brown sugar	*5 oz light soft brown sugar*
2 eggs	*2 eggs*
2 × 15 ml spoons golden syrup	*2 tablespoons golden syrup*
125 ml corn or vegetable oil	*scant ¼ pint corn or vegetable oil*
125 ml milk	*scant ¼ pint milk*

Chocolate icing:	Chocolate icing:
50 g plain chocolate	*2 oz plain chocolate*
25 g butter	*1 oz butter*
few drops of vanilla essence	*few drops of vanilla essence*
25 g icing sugar, sifted	*1 oz icing sugar, sifted*
25 g walnuts, roughly chopped	*1 oz walnuts, roughly chopped*

Preparation time: 10 minutes
Cooking time: 1–1¼ hours
Oven: 160°C, 325°F, Gas Mark 3

Sift the flour, cocoa, baking powder and soda into a bowl, then mix in the sugar. Make a well in the centre of the dry ingredients and add the eggs and golden syrup. Gradually add the oil and milk, beating continuously to give a smooth batter. A hand-held electric mixer is ideal for this job.

Pour into a greased and lined 18 cm/7 inch round or square cake tin and bake in a preheated oven for 1–1¼ hours or until well risen and firm to the touch. A skewer inserted in the centre of the cake should come out clean. Turn on to a wire rack and leave to cool.

To make the icing, melt the chocolate in a heatproof basin over a pan of hot water. Stir in the butter, vanilla essence and icing sugar. Remove from the heat and leave until the icing begins to thicken, then spread quickly over the top of the cake. Sprinkle with the chopped walnuts and leave to set.

Speedy chocolate cake, Coffee fudge cake

Rich fruit cake

Metric	Imperial
225 g currants	8 oz currants
225 g sultanas	8 oz sultanas
225 g seedless raisins	8 oz seedless raisins
100 g chopped mixed peel	4 oz chopped mixed peel
50 g blanched almonds, chopped	2 oz blanched almonds, chopped
grated rind of 1 orange or lemon	grated rind of 1 orange or lemon
50 g glacé cherries, quartered, rinsed and dried thoroughly	2 oz glacé cherries, quartered, rinsed and dried thoroughly
200 g plain flour	8 oz plain flour
pinch of salt	pinch of salt
1 × 5 ml spoon mixed spice	1 teaspoon mixed spice
1 × 2.5 ml spoon ground cinnamon	½ teaspoon ground cinnamon
200 g butter or margarine	8 oz butter or margarine
150 g light soft brown sugar	6 oz light soft brown sugar
4 eggs (sizes 1, 2)	4 eggs (sizes 1, 2)
1 × 15 ml spoon brandy or sherry	1 tablespoon brandy or sherry
1 × 15 ml spoon black treacle	1 tablespoon black treacle

Preparation time: 20 minutes
Cooking time: 3½–3¾ hours
Oven: 150°C, 300°F, Gas Mark 2

This makes a delicious cake as it is or turn it into a Christmas or special celebration cake by coating it in 500 g/1¼ lb bought or home-made marzipan and royal icing made with 700 g/1½ lb icing sugar, which is enough for a simple decoration as well. Before doing this a little extra alcohol may be spooned over the base of the cake, after a few holes have been made with a skewer.

Grease and line a 20 cm/8 inch deep round cake tin. Mix together the dried fruits, peel, almonds, fruit rind and glacé cherries. Sift the flour with the salt and the spices. Cream the butter or margarine until soft, then add the sugar and continue creaming until light and fluffy and very pale in colour. Beat in the eggs one at a time, adding a spoonful of flour in between. Fold in the remaining flour, then the brandy or sherry and treacle. Mix in the dried fruit thoroughly.
Turn into the cake tin, level the top and make a slight hollow in the centre with the back of a spoon. Tie a treble thickness of newspaper round the outside of the tin and bake in a preheated cool oven for 3½–3¾ hours or until the cake is firm to the touch and a skewer inserted comes out clean. Leave to cool in the tin for about 15 minutes, then turn out on to a wire rack. When cold, store wrapped in foil, for up to 1 month.

Royal icing

Metric	Imperial
3 egg whites	3 egg whites
about 700 g icing sugar, sifted	about 1½ lb icing sugar, sifted
1 × 15 ml spoon lemon juice	1 tablespoon lemon juice
2 × 5 ml spoons glycerine (optional)	2 teaspoons glycerine (optional)

Preparation time: about 15 minutes, plus time for the icing to stand, and set between layers.

Beat the egg whites until frothy, then gradually beat in half the sugar using a wooden spoon. Add the lemon juice and glycerine if using, then beat in half the remaining sugar. Continue beating until smooth and very white. Gradually beat in enough of the remaining sugar to give a soft peak consistency. Put the icing in an airtight container, or cover with a damp cloth, and leave to stand for 1 hour or so, if possible. This allows most of the air bubbles to disperse.
To royal ice the cake for Christmas, first flat-ice the top of the cake, pulling an icing ruler across it to give a smooth, even surface. Two thin layers of icing are better than one thick layer, but leave the first layer for a few hours to set before applying a second.
Reserve a little icing for decoration in an airtight container, then add a little more icing sugar to the remainder to give a stiffer consistency suitable for rough icing. Spread all round the sides of the cake, allowing it to tip slightly over the top edge, then pull up into peaks using a round-bladed knife; leave to set. Draw a star about 10 cm/4 inches across on stiff paper and cut out. Position the template on the centre top of the cake and trace around it with icing using a writing nozzle. Remove the template. When the outline is set over-pipe. Tint a little icing yellow and outline each point of the star. Carefully attach a red candle in the centre of the star with stiff icing and decorate around the base with holly leaves and berries (either bought or made from marzipan). Finish with holy leaves and berries between each point of the star.

Royal icing, Rich fruit cake, Marzipan

102

Marzipan

Metric
275 g ground almonds
150 g caster sugar
150 g icing sugar, sifted
1 × 5 ml spoon lemon juice
few drops of almond
    essence
1 egg or 2 egg yolks
apricot jam, melted
    and sieved, to secure
    the marzipan

Imperial
10 oz ground almonds
5 oz caster sugar
5 oz icing sugar, sifted
1 teaspoon lemon juice
few drops of almond
    essence
1 egg or 2 egg yolks
apricot jam, melted
    and sieved, to secure
    the marzipan

Preparation time: about 10 minutes

Mix the ground almonds with the sugars and make a well in the centre. Add the lemon juice, almond essence and sufficient egg or egg yolks to mix to a firm but manageable consistency. Knead on a lightly sugared surface until smooth, and keep tightly wrapped in polythene or foil until required.

To cover a cake with marzipan, measure around the outside of the cake with a piece of string, and then the depth of it. Roll out two-thirds of the marzipan into a strip half this length and twice as wide as the depth of the cake; trim and cut in half lengthwise. Roll out the remaining marzipan into a circle to fit the top. Brush the cake all over with melted apricot jam and place on a cake board. First position the marzipan around the sides, pressing the joins well together. Put on the top, again pressing the edges together. Rub a little icing sugar all over the marzipan and leave for several days to set.

Chelsea buns

Metric	Imperial
225 g strong plain white flour	8 oz strong plain white flour
15 g fresh yeast or 1½ × 5 ml spoons dried yeast	½ oz fresh yeast or 1½ teaspoons dried yeast
1 × 5 ml spoon caster sugar	1 teaspoon caster sugar
100 ml warm milk	4 fl oz warm milk
1 × 2.5 ml spoon salt	½ teaspoon salt
15 g butter	½ oz butter
1 egg (sizes 6, 7), beaten	1 egg (sizes 6, 7), beaten
50 g butter or margarine, melted	2 oz butter or margarine, melted
50 g currants	2 oz currants
50 g seedless raisins	2 oz seedless raisins
25 g chopped mixed peel	1 oz chopped mixed peel
1 × 2.5 ml spoon ground cinnamon	½ teaspoon ground cinnamon
50 g soft brown sugar	2 oz soft brown sugar
clear honey or golden syrup, to glaze	clear honey or golden syrup, to glaze

Preparation time: 25 minues, plus rising time
Cooking time: 30–35 minutes
Oven: 190°C, 375°F, Gas Mark 5

Sift 50 g/2 oz of the flour into a bowl. Add the yeast (fresh or dried), caster sugar and milk, mix to a smooth batter and leave in a warm place for about 20 minutes or until frothy.

Sift the remaining flour and the salt into a bowl and rub in the butter. Add to the yeast batter together with the beaten egg and mix to form a soft dough which leaves the sides of the bowl clean. Turn on to a lightly floured surface and knead for 5 minutes or until smooth and no longer sticky.

Shape the dough into a ball, place in an oiled polythene bag and tie loosely at the top. Leave to rise in a warm place for 1–1½ hours or until doubled in size.

Remove the dough from the bag, knock back and knead lightly. Roll out to an oblong 30 × 24 cm/ 12 × 9 inches and brush liberally with the melted butter or margarine. Mix the dried fruits, peel, cinnamon and brown sugar together and sprinkle over the dough. Begin at a short end and roll it up carefully into a neat roll. Seal the edge with water. Cut into nine even-sized slices and place in a greased 20 cm/7 inch square cake tin, cut sides down, so they almost touch. Cover with oiled polythene and leave to rise in a warm place for about 30 minutes or until doubled in size.

Bake in a preheated oven for 30–35 minutes or until well risen and golden brown. Turn on to a wire rack, still in one piece, and brush with honey or syrup.
Makes 9

Apple cake

Metric	Imperial
225 g plain flour	8 oz plain flour
1 × 2.5 ml spoon ground cinnamon	½ teaspoon ground cinnamon
1 × 2.5 ml spoon mixed spice (optional)	½ teaspoon mixed spice (optional)
1 × 2.5 ml spoon bicarbonate of soda	½ teaspoon bicarbonate of soda
100 g butter or margarine	4 oz butter or margarine
150 g light soft brown or caster sugar	6 oz light soft brown or caster sugar
2 eggs	2 eggs
100 g currants	4 oz currants
175 g sultanas	6 oz sultanas
50 g walnuts, chopped	2 oz walnuts, chopped
225 g cooking apples, peeled, cored and coarsely grated	8 oz cooking apples, peeled, cored and coarsely grated
grated rind of 1 lemon	grated rind of 1 lemon

Preparation time: 10 minutes
Cooking time: 1¼–1½ hours
Oven: 180°C, 350°F, Gas Mark 4

Sift the flour, spices and soda together. In a separate bowl cream together the butter or margarine and sugar until light and fluffy and pale in colour. Beat in the eggs one at a time, following each with a spoonful of the flour mixture. Fold in the remaining flour followed by the currants, sultanas, walnuts and finally the grated apple and lemon rind.

Turn into a greased and lined 20 cm/8 inch round cake tin, level the top and bake in a preheated oven for 1¼–1½ hours or until the cake is firm to the touch and a skewer inserted in the centre comes out clean. Turn out and cool on a wire rack.

Variation:
Use 50 g/2 oz chopped mixed peel in place of the walnuts.

Chelsea buns, Apple cake

Cream slices

Metric	Imperial
225 g puff pastry	8 oz puff pastry

Glacé icing:

100 g icing sugar	4 oz icing sugar
1–2 × 15 ml spoons warm water or lemon juice	1–2 tablespoons warm water or lemon juice

Filling:

6 × 15 ml spoons raspberry jam	6 tablespoons raspberry jam
150 ml spoons double cream, lightly whipped	¼ pint double cream, lightly whipped

Preparation time: 15 minutes
Cooking time: 15–20 minutes
Oven: 230°C, 450°F, Gas Mark 8

Roll out the dough on a floured surface to a rectangle and trim to 30 × 25 cm/12 × 10 inches. Cut in half lengthwise; for one large cream slice transfer the two rectangles to dampened or lightly greased baking sheets. For individual slices, cut each rectangle of dough into 13 × 5 cm/5 × 2 inch strips and place on baking sheets. Leave to rest for 10 minutes, then bake in a preheated oven for 15–20 minutes or until well risen and golden brown. Cool on wire racks. Select the best large piece, or 6 small pieces, of pastry to be iced for the tops.

To make the glacé icing, sift the icing sugar into a bowl and beat in sufficient warm water or lemon juice to give a thick coating consistency. Spread the white icing evenly over the best pieces of pastry. Leave to set.

To assemble the cream slices, spread the pastry base or bases with jam and then with whipped cream and position the tops, pressing down gently to given an even shape. The large cream slice can then be cut carefully into six slices.
Makes 6

Variations:

To decorate the slices with pink feathering, remove about 1 × 15 ml spoon/1 tablespoon icing and tint it with pink food colouring. Put this into a greaseproof icing bag. Quickly cut the tip off the icing bag and pipe straight lines of pink across the white icing at 1 cm/½ inch intervals. Take a skewer and quickly draw across the lines at 1 cm/½ inch intervals, first from one end and then the other.

A little chocolate glacé icing may be used in place of pink for the feathering. Sift 1 × 15 ml spoon/1 tablespoon cocoa powder in with the icing sugar and mix with black coffee or water.

The tops may be sprinkled with toasted flaked almonds.

Victoria sandwich cake

Metric	Imperial
100 g butter or margarine	4 oz butter or margarine
100 g caster sugar	4 oz caster sugar
2 eggs	2 eggs
100 g self-raising flour, sifted	4 oz self-raising flour, sifted
1 × 15 ml spoon cold water (optional)	1 tablespoon cold water (optional)
few drops of vanilla essence (optional)	few drops of vanilla essence (optional)
3–4 × 15 ml spoons raspberry, strawberry or other flavour jam, to fill	3–4 tablespoons raspberry, strawberry or other flavour jam, to fill
icing or caster sugar for dredging	icing or caster sugar for dredging

Preparation time: 10 minutes
Cooking time: about 20 minutes
Oven: 190°C, 375°F, Gas Mark 5

Grease two 18 cm/7 inch sandwich tins and line the bases with greased greaseproof paper. Cream together the butter or margarine and sugar until very light and fluffy, and pale in colour. Beat in the eggs one at a time following each with a spoonful of flour. Fold in the remaining flour with a metal spoon, followed by the water and essence, if used. Although the flour should be thoroughly incorporated do not over-mix or the cake will not rise so well.

Divide between the tins, level the tops and bake in a preheated oven for 15–20 minutes or until well risen, golden brown and firm to the touch. Turn out on to wire racks and leave to cool.

When cold, sandwich the cakes together with the jam and dredge the top with sugar.

Variations:

Cream and jam sandwich cake: Spread a layer of whipped cream over the jam before sandwiching the cakes together. Store any left-over cake in the refrigerator.

Coffee sandwich cake: Replace the water with 1 × 15 ml spoon/1 tablespoon coffee essence and omit other flavourings. Fill with Coffee Butter Cream (see right).

Chocolate sandwich cake: Replace 20 g/¾ oz of the flour with sifted cocoa powder and flavour with vanilla essence. Fill with Chocolate or Butter Cream (see right).

Lemon or orange sandwich cake: Add the finely grated rind of 1 lemon or orange and omit all the other flavourings. Sandwich together with lemon curd or orange marmalade and a layer of whipped cream, if liked, or Butter Cream (see right).

Butter cream

Metric	Imperial
50 g butter or soft (tub) margarine	*2 oz butter or soft (tub) margarine*
75–100 g icing sugar, sifted	*3–4 oz icing sugar, sifted*
few drops of vanilla essence	*few drops of vanilla essence*
about 1 × 15 ml spoon milk or evaporated milk	*about 1 tablespoon milk or evaporated milk*

Preparation time: about 10 minutes

Cream the fat until soft, then beat in the sugar a little at a time, adding the vanilla essence and sufficient milk to give a fairly firm but spreading consistency. Use to fill the sandwich cake.
To fill and ice the top of the cake double the quantities.

Variations:

Coffee butter cream: Omit the vanilla essence and replace the milk with coffee essence or strong black coffee.

Chocolate butter cream: Either add 1 × 15 ml spoon/1 tablespoon sifted cocoa powder or 25 g/1 oz melted chocolate to the icing.

Lemon or orange butter cream: Omit the vanilla essence, replace the milk with lemon or orange juice and add the finely grated rind of 1 lemon or orange.

Cream slices, Victoria sandwich cake filled with whipped cream

Outdoor Eating

A meal in the garden, a picnic or a packed lunch are all occasions which require a certain type of food – mainly something that is both easy to transport and easy to eat. Barbecues are now popular and, weather permitting, make cooking food out of doors enjoyable. Transporting difficulties have been solved with foil and plastic containers made specially for the job, and there are many foods particularly suitable for a moveable feast. For example, food encased in pastry is hard to beat and with a tomato, a piece of cheese and an apple you have an interesting and well-balanced meal.

Potted turkey

Metric	Imperial
225 g cooked turkey meat	8 oz cooked turkey meat
100 g butter	4 oz butter
1 onion, peeled and very finely chopped	1 onion, peeled and very finely chopped
1–2 garlic cloves, peeled and crushed	1–2 garlic cloves, peeled and crushed
2 × 15 ml spoons sherry or port	2 tablespoons sherry or port
about 4 × 15 ml spoons stock	about 4 tablespoons stock
salt	salt
freshly ground black pepper	freshly ground black pepper
pinch of ground mace or ground nutmeg	pinch of ground mace or ground nutmeg
pinch of dried mixed herbs (optional)	pinch of dried mixed herbs (optional)

To garnish:	To garnish:
stuffed olives	stuffed olives
tomatoes	tomatoes

Preparation time: 20 minutes, plus chilling time
Cooking time: 5 minutes

Cooked beef, chicken meat, ham or game can also be 'potted' in this way.

Mince the turkey meat finely twice. Melt half the butter in a frying pan, add the onion and garlic and fry gently until soft and lightly coloured. Stir in the minced turkey followed by the sherry or port and sufficient stock just to moisten. Season to taste with salt, pepper and mace or nutmeg and add the herbs. Press the turkey into a lightly greased dish or several individual ones and level the tops. Chill until firm.
Melt the remaining butter and pour a thin layer over the potted turkey. Chill until required. Serve garnished with stuffed olives and slices of tomato.
Potted turkey will keep for 2–3 days in the refrigerator but not longer for it does not contain any preservative. Serves 4–6

Potted turkey, Raised picnic pie

Raised picnic pie

Metric	Imperial
400 g plain flour	1 lb plain flour
1 × 5 ml spoon salt	1 teaspoon salt
100 g lard	4 oz lard
150 ml water	¼ pint water
4 × 15 ml spoons milk	4 tablespoons milk

Filling:	Filling:
450 g chicken meat, chopped	1 lb chicken meat, chopped
225 g cooked ham or bacon, chopped	8 oz cooked ham or bacon, chopped
1 small onion, peeled and finely chopped	1 small onion, peeled and finely chopped
salt	salt
freshly ground black pepper	freshly ground black pepper
1 × 2.5 ml spoon dried thyme (optional)	½ teaspoon dried thyme (optional)
225–350 g sausage meat	8–12 oz sausage meat
beaten egg or milk, to glaze	beaten egg or milk, to glaze
1 × 15 ml spoon powdered gelatine	1 tablespoon powdered gelatine
300 ml chicken stock	¼ pint chicken stock

Preparation time: 30 minutes
Cooking time: about 2 hours
Oven: 200°C, 400°F, Gas Mark 6
          160°C, 325°F, Gas Mark 3

To make the pastry, sift the flour and salt into a bowl. Put the lard into a saucepan with the water and milk, heat gently until the lard melts, then bring to the boil. Pour all at once into the flour and mix to form a pliable dough, then knead lightly.
Remove three-quarters of the dough to a lightly floured surface, keeping the remainder warm in the bowl covered with a cloth. Roll out the dough to a round and use to line a lightly greased 18 cm/7 inch loose-bottomed round cake tin or game pie mould.
Mix together the chicken, ham or bacon and onion and season with salt, pepper and thyme. Spread the sausage meat in a thin layer in the tin or mould, then fill up with the meat mixture. Roll out the reserved dough for a lid, dampen the edges and position. Press well together, trim off excess dough and crimp. Make a hole in the centre and decorate around it with dough leaves. Glaze the top and cook in a preheated oven for 30 minutes. Reduce the temperature and cook for 1–1¼ hours, putting greaseproof paper over the pie when sufficiently browned. Cool on a wire rack. Dissolve the gelatine in the stock in a heatproof basin over a pan of hot water. Pour through the hole in the centre of the pie. Chill thoroughly before serving.

Chicken puffs

Metric	Imperial
40 g butter or margarine	1½ oz butter or margarine
1 small onion, peeled and finely chopped	1 small onion, peeled and finely chopped
50 g mushrooms, chopped	2 oz mushrooms, chopped
25 g plain flour	1 oz plain flour
150 ml chicken stock	¼ pint chicken stock
4 × 15 ml spoons milk	4 tablespoons milk
pinch of grated nutmeg	pinch of grated nutmeg
175 g cooked chicken meat, finely chopped	6 oz cooked chicken meat, finely chopped
10–12 stuffed green olives, sliced	10–12 stuffed green olives, sliced
salt	salt
freshly ground black pepper	freshly ground black pepper
225 g puff pastry	8 oz puff pastry
beaten egg or milk, to glaze	beaten egg or milk, to glaze

Preparation time: 20–25 minutes
Cooking time: about 30 minutes
Oven: 220°C, 425°F, Gas Mark 7

Cooked turkey meat, ham or beef or a mixture of meats may also be used for the puffs, as may canned tuna fish or salmon.

Melt the butter or margarine in a saucepan, add the onion and fry until soft. Add the mushrooms and continue frying for a minute or so longer. Stir in the flour and cook for 1 minute then gradually stir in the stock and milk and bring to the boil. Simmer for 2 minutes. Remove from the heat and stir in the nutmeg, chicken, olives, salt and pepper. Cool.
Roll out about one-third of the dough thinly and cut into four 13 cm/5 inch rounds; place on a dampened or lightly greased baking sheet. Spoon the filling on to the rounds, leaving a 2 cm/¾ inch margin all round. Roll out the remaining dough and cut into four 17 cm/6½ inch rounds. Brush the edges of the rounds on the baking sheet with water and carefully position the larger rounds on top. Press the edges very well together, then knock up or flake the edges and make a slit in the top of each puff. Brush all over with beaten egg or milk, decorate the tops with dough leaves and glaze again.
Cook in a preheated oven for 20–25 minutes or until well risen, golden brown and puffy. Remove to a wire rack to cool. Serve warm or cold with a salad.

Sausage and salami plait

Metric	Imperial
450 g sausage meat	1 lb sausage meat
100 g salami, finely chopped	4 oz salami, finely chopped
100 g lean bacon, rind removed, chopped	4 oz lean bacon, rind removed, chopped
1 small onion, peeled and finely chopped	1 small onion, peeled and finely chopped
100 g mushrooms, chopped	4 oz mushrooms, chopped
salt	salt
freshly ground black pepper	freshly ground black pepper
350 g puff pastry or 1 × 375 g packet frozen puff pastry, thawed	12 oz puff pastry or 1 × 13 oz packet frozen puff pastry, thawed
beaten egg, to glaze	beaten egg, to glaze

Preparation time: 20 minutes
Cooking time: 40–45 minutes
Oven: 220°C, 425°F, Gas Mark 7
180°C, 350°F, Gas Mark 4

Place the sausage meat in a bowl and knead in the salami, bacon, onion, mushrooms and salt and pepper to taste. Roll out the pastry on a floured surface and trim to a 25 cm/12 inch square. Put the filling down the centre of the square to within 2.5 cm/1 inch of the top and bottom and about 10 cm/4 inches from the sides. Using a sharp knife cut diagonal slashes 2.5 cm/1 inch away from the filling to the sides and 2.5–4 cm/1–1½ inches apart.
Fold the top and bottom over the filling and brush with some of the beaten egg. Carefully plait the strips from the sides over the filling, taking first one from one side and then one from the other side and brushing each with egg as it is positioned. The filling should be completely enclosed.
Place on a baking sheet, brush all over with beaten egg and cook in a preheated oven for 20 minutes. Reduce the temperature and continue baking for 20–25 minutes, laying a piece of greaseproof paper over the plait when it is sufficiently browned. Serve cold, sliced, with salads.

Sausage and salami plait, Cidered cheese fondue, Chicken puffs

Cidered cheese fondue

Preparation time: 10 minutes
Cooking time: about 15 minutes

Metric
1 garlic clove, peeled and
  crushed
450 g mature Cheddar
  cheese, finely grated
50 g Gruyère cheese,
  grated
600 ml dry cider
25 g cornflour
salt
freshly ground black
  pepper
freshly grated nutmeg

To serve:
French bread cubes,
  warmed
carrot sticks
celery sticks

Imperial
1 garlic clove, peeled and
  crushed
1 lb mature Cheddar
  cheese, finely grated
2 oz Gruyère cheese,
  grated
1 pint dry cider
1 oz cornflour
salt
freshly ground black
  pepper
freshly grated nutmeg

To serve:
French bread cubes,
  warmed
carrot sticks
celery sticks

If you have a fondue set with a spirit burner, take the whole thing to the table; it will keep the fondue hot and prevent it from setting. If you are using a casserole, reheat gently from time to time on the stove as necessary.

Rub the garlic around the inside of a flameproof casserole or cheese fondue pot and leave the garlic in the pot. Add the cheese and all but 3 × 15 ml spoons/ 3 tablespoons of the cider and mix well. Heat very gently until the cheese has melted, stirring frequently; do not allow to boil.

Dissolve the cornflour in the remaining cider, add a little of the cheese mixture to it, then return it all to the pan. Bring slowly to the boil, stirring constantly until the mixture has thickened. Add salt, pepper and nutmeg and serve at once with cubes of warmed French bread and carrot and celery sticks to dip in the cheese fondue.

Skewered lamb with wine and garlic

Metric	Imperial
1 onion, peeled and chopped	1 onion, peeled and chopped
1 garlic clove, peeled and crushed	1 garlic clove, peeled and crushed
2 × 5 ml spoons dried mixed herbs	2 teaspoons dried mixed herbs
4 × 15 ml spoons oil	4 tablespoons oil
6 × 15 ml spoons red wine	6 tablespoons red wine
1 × 15 ml spoon lemon juice	1 tablespoon lemon juice
salt	salt
freshly ground black pepper	freshly ground black pepper
750 g top of leg of lamb, cut into 2.5 cm cubes	1½ lb top of leg of lamb, cut into 1 inch cubes
8 streaky bacon rashers, rind removed, rolled	8 streaky bacon rashers, rind removed, rolled
8 mushrooms	8 mushrooms

Preparation time: 15 minutes, plus marinating time
Cooking time: 15–20 minutes

The longer the meat is left in the marinade the better the flavours will permeate it. For this reason the marinating ingredients and meat can be easily combined the night before.

Put the onion, garlic, herbs, oil, wine, lemon juice and salt and pepper to taste into a bowl and mix well. Add the lamb cubes, cover the bowl with cling film or foil and leave to marinate for several hours, turning the meat once or twice.
When required thread the lamb, bacon rolls and mushrooms alternately on to long skewers. Reserve the marinade.
To cook outdoors on a barbecue allow 5–10 minutes cooking on each side, depending on the heat, and brush once or twice with the marinade. If cooking under the grill use a medium heat and allow 15–20 minutes, basting and turning once or twice.
Serve with boiled rice or baked jacket potatoes and a Red Bean and Carrot Salad (page 61).

Turkey kebabs with devilled sauce

Metric	Imperial
450 g turkey meat, dark or white, cut into 2.5 cm cubes	1 lb turkey meat, dark or white, cut into 1 inch cubes
8 lean bacon rashers, rind removed, rolled	8 lean bacon rashers, rind removed, rolled
8 onion wedges, or 4 baby onions, halved	8 onion wedges, or 4 baby onions, halved
2 × 15 ml spoons apricot jam	2 tablespoons apricot jam
4 × 15 ml spoons tomato ketchup	4 tablespoons tomato ketchup
1 × 15 ml spoon soy sauce	1 tablespoon soy sauce
1–2 × 5 ml spoons Dijon mustard	1–2 teaspoons Dijon mustard
1 garlic clove, peeled and crushed	1 garlic clove, peeled and crushed
1 × 15 ml spoon Worcestershire sauce	1 tablespoon Worcestershire sauce
1 × 2.5 ml spoon grated lemon rind	½ teaspoon grated lemon rind
1 × 15 ml spoon lemon juice	1 tablespoon lemon juice
2 × 15 ml spoons oil	2 tablespoons oil
pinch of cayenne pepper	pinch of cayenne pepper
salt	salt
freshly ground black pepper	freshly ground black pepper

Preparation time: about 15 minutes
Cooking time: about 20 minutes

Thread the turkey cubes on to 4 long skewers alternating with the bacon rolls and onions. Put the jam, ketchup, soy sauce, mustard, garlic, Worcestershire sauce, lemon rind and juice, oil, cayenne and salt and pepper to taste in a pan and bring just to the boil. Remove quickly from the heat and brush the sauce all over the kebabs.
Cook on a hot barbecue or under a preheated moderate grill for 8–10 minutes on each side or until cooked through. Brush at least once more with the sauce during cooking. Serve with a Sweetcorn and Bean-Sprout Salad (page 61) and baked jacket potatoes or hot crispy bread.

Devilled sauce, Turkey kebabs, Skewered lamb

Poldark pasties

Metric	Imperial
200 g plain flour	8 oz plain flour
pinch of salt	pinch of salt
50 g butter or margarine	2 oz butter or margarine
50 g lard	2 oz lard
cold water, to mix	cold water, to mix

Filling:	Filling:
25 g butter or margarine	1 oz butter or margarine
1 small onion, peeled and chopped	1 small onion, peeled and chopped
1 × 15 ml spoon plain flour	1 tablespoon plain flour
150 ml milk	¼ pint milk
2 hard-boiled eggs, chopped	2 hard-boiled eggs, chopped
2 × 15 ml spoons chopped fresh parsley	2 tablespoons chopped fresh parsley
225 g smoked mackerel fillets, skinned and flaked	8 oz smoked mackerel fillets, skinned and flaked
salt	salt
freshly ground black pepper	freshly ground black pepper
beaten egg or milk, to glaze	beaten egg or milk, to glaze

Preparation time: 20 minutes
Cooking time: 20–25 minutes
Oven: 200°C, 400°F, Gas Mark 6

To make the pastry, sift the flour and salt into a bowl and rub in the fats until the mixture resembles fine breadcrumbs. Add sufficient water to bind to a pliable dough. Wrap in polythene or foil and chill.
To make the filling, melt the butter or margarine in a saucepan, add the onion and fry gently until soft. Stir in the flour and cook for 1 minute, then gradually stir in the milk and bring to the boil. Simmer for 1 minute. Remove from the heat and stir in the eggs, parsley, mackerel and salt and pepper. Leave to cool. Roll out the dough and cut into 4 rounds, each 18–20 cm/7–8 inches across. Divide the filling between the rounds, placing it in the centre. Dampen the dough edges and bring them together at the top. Press very well together and crimp, then place on a dampened or lightly greased baking sheet. Brush all over with beaten egg or milk and cook in a preheated oven for 20–25 minutes or until golden brown. Serve hot or cold, with a salad.

Pork and beef burgers with barbecue sauce

Metric	Imperial
350 g lean pork, minced	12 oz lean pork, minced
225 g minced beef	8 oz minced beef
1 onion, peeled and finely chopped	1 onion, peeled and finely chopped
1 garlic clove, peeled and crushed	1 garlic clove, peeled and crushed
3 × 15 ml spoons fresh breadcrumbs	3 tablespoons fresh breadcrumbs
salt	salt
freshly ground black pepper	freshly ground black pepper
1 egg yolk	1 egg yolk

Barbecue sauce:	Barbecue sauce:
300 ml tomato ketchup	½ pint tomato ketchup
25 g butter or margarine	1 oz butter or margarine
4 × 15 ml spoons vinegar	4 tablespoons vinegar
pinch of chilli powder	pinch of chilli powder
2 × 5 ml spoons brown sugar	2 teaspoons brown sugar
1 × 2.5 ml spoon celery salt	½ teaspoon celery salt
1 × 2.5 ml spoon dried mixed herbs	½ teaspoon dried mixed herbs
1 garlic clove, peeled and crushed	1 garlic clove, peeled and crushed
2 × 15 ml spoons grated onion	2 tablespoons grated onion
2–3 tomatoes, skinned and chopped	2–3 tomatoes, skinned and chopped
oil (optional)	oil (optional)
watercress, to garnish	watercress, to garnish

Preparation time: 20 minutes
Cooking time: about 15 minutes

Chilli powder is very hot, so use it cautiously.

Combine the pork, beef, onion, garlic, breadcrumbs and salt and pepper, and bind with the egg yolk. Divide into 4 or 8 and shape into flat round cakes.
To make the sauce, put all the ingredients, except the tomatoes, into a pan, bring to the boil, cover and simmer gently for 10–15 minutes, stirring occasionally. Stir in the tomatoes and simmer for 2 minutes.
To cook the burgers on a barbecue, first brush them lightly with oil, then cook over a moderate heat for 5–8 minutes on each side, brushing each side with the barbecue sauce halfway through cooking time. Alternatively, cook under a preheated moderate grill, without brushing first with oil, for the same time each side. Serve with the remaining sauce, reheated, and garnished with watercress.

Ham and tongue mousses

Metric
25 g butter or margarine
25 g plain flour
300 ml milk
2 eggs, separated
large pinch of dry mustard
4 × 5 ml spoons powdered
  gelatine
2 × 15 ml spoons water
100 g cooked ham, minced
100 g cooked tongue,
  minced
large pinch dried tarragon
150 ml soured cream
salt
freshly ground black
  pepper

To garnish:
slices of hard-boiled egg
mustard and cress

Imperial
1 oz butter or margarine
1 oz plain flour
½ pint milk
2 eggs, separated
large pinch of dry mustard
4 teaspoons powdered
  gelatine
2 tablespoons water
4 oz cooked ham, minced
4 oz cooked tongue,
  minced
large pinch dried tarragon
¼ pint soured cream
salt
freshly ground black
  pepper

To garnish:
slices of hard-boiled egg
mustard and cress

Preparation time: 25 minutes, plus setting time

Ham or tongue alone may be used for this mousse.

Melt the butter or margarine in a pan, stir in the flour and cook for 1 minute. Gradually stir in the milk over a low heat and bring to the boil. Simmer for 2 minutes. Remove from the heat and stir in the egg yolks and dry mustard.
Dissolve the gelatine in the water in a heatproof basin over a pan of hot water, then stir into the sauce. Cover closely and leave until cold and beginning to thicken. Quickly stir the ham, tongue, herbs and soured cream into the thickened sauce and season to taste with salt and pepper. Whisk the egg whites until stiff and fold through the mixture. Pour into four or five individual dishes or a large bowl and chill until set. Serve garnished with slices of hard-boiled egg and mustard and cress.
Serves 4–5

Ham and tongue mousses, Pork and beef burgers with barbecue sauce, Poldark pasties

115

Menus for the Family

The following menus, which are suitable for a more special lunch or dinner, allow you to make the starter and dessert well in advance – leaving only the main course and vegetables to keep an eye on nearer the time; the starter to assemble and the dessert to decorate.

Getting organized

The day before, prepare the pork and potatoes ready for cooking and make the dessert. On the day make the salami cones early in the morning, cover and refrigerate; arrange them on the salad at the last minute. Decorate the dessert shortly before your guests arrive. Serve French beans and leeks au gratin with the main course. Cover cooked leeks with a cheese sauce, scatter grated cheese or breadcrumbs on top and brown under the grill.

Cheese and salami salad

Metric	Imperial
350 g full fat soft cheese	*12 oz full fat soft cheese*
50 g butter, softened	*2 oz butter, softened*
1–2 garlic cloves, peeled and crushed	*1–2 garlic cloves, peeled and crushed*
1–2 × 15 ml spoons cream or top of the milk	*1–2 tablespoons cream or top of the milk*
salt	*salt*
freshly ground black pepper	*freshly ground black pepper*
1 × 15 ml spoon capers, chopped (optional)	*1 tablespoon capers, chopped (optional)*
16–24 slices of salami	*16–24 slices of salami*
lettuce leaves	*lettuce leaves*

To garnish:	To garnish:
black olives	*black olives*
mustard and cress	*mustard and cress*

Preparation time: about 20 minutes

If the salami slices are large 2 cones each will be sufficient; if small allow 3 each.

Beat the cheese until soft and creamy, then beat in the butter, garlic, cream, salt and pepper to give a smooth piping consistency. Add the capers and put into a piping bag fitted with a large star nozzle. Remove the skin from around the edge of the salami and roll each slice into a cone. Pipe a whirl of the cheese mixture carefully into each cone.
Place 2 or 3 cones on a few lettuce leaves, Garnish with an olive and mustard and cress.

Roast stuffed pork with fantail potatoes

Metric

1 × 1½–1¾ kg loin of
  pork, boned
4 lean back bacon rashers,
  rind removed
100 g liver pâté
1 garlic clove, peeled and
  crushed
1 × 2.5 ml spoon dried
  mixed herbs (optional)
oil or dripping
salt
8–16 medium potatoes,
  peeled
1–2 × 15 ml spoons plain
  flour
450 ml beef stock
2 × 5 ml spoons tomato
  purée
dash of Worcestershire
  sauce
freshly ground black
  pepper
watercress, to garnish

Imperial

1 × 3½–4 lb loin of pork,
  boned
4 lean back bacon rashers,
  rind removed
4 oz liver pâté
1 garlic clove, peeled and
  crushed
½ teaspoon dried mixed
  herbs (optional)
oil or dripping
salt
8–16 medium potatoes,
  peeled
1–2 tablespoons plain
  flour
¾ pint beef stock
2 teaspoons tomato
  purée
dash of Worcestershire
  sauce
freshly ground black
  pepper
watercress, to garnish

Preparation time: 10 minutes
Cooking time: 2½–3 hours
Oven: 190°C, 375°F, Gas Mark 5

Lay the pork flat and cut the flesh a little if necessary to open it out for the stuffing. Lay the bacon rashers evenly over the surface. Mix together the pâté, garlic and herbs, if used, and spread down the length of the pork over the bacon. Roll up the joint carefully, enclosing the stuffing, and tie into shape with string. Weigh the joint, then place it in a roasting tin. Rub all over with oil or dripping, then rub in a layer of salt. Roast in a preheated oven, allowing 30–35 minutes per 450 g/1 lb plus 30 minutes over.

After 1 hour make the fantail potatoes. Slice the potatoes thinly, almost through to the base but leaving a hinge on the bottom. Add the potatoes to the tin and baste the joint and potatoes with the fat in the tin. Continue roasting for the remainder of cooking time, basting the potatoes once or twice more until they are well browned and opened out and the pork is cooked through with a crisp crackling. Remove to a heated serving dish.

Drain off all but 1 × 15 ml spoon/1 tablespoon fat from the tin and stir in the flour. Add the stock, tomato purée, Worcestershire sauce and salt and pepper to taste and bring to the boil, stirring. Boil for 2 minutes. Strain into a jug. Serve the pork and fantail potatoes garnished with watercress.

Jellied grape bavarois

Metric

2 lime jelly tablets
2 × 15 ml spoons lemon
  juice
175 g black grapes, halved
  and pipped
225 g green grapes, halved
  and pipped
250–275 ml milk
2 × 15 ml spoons custard
  powder
1 × 15 ml spoon sugar
300 ml soured cream

To decorate:
1 egg white
175 g black grapes
caster sugar
whipped cream

Imperial

2 lime jelly tablets
2 tablespoons lemon
  juice
6 oz black grapes, halved
  and pipped
8 oz green grapes, halved
  and pipped
½ pint milk
2 tablespoons custard
  powder
1 tablespoon sugar
½ pint soured cream

To decorate:
1 egg white
6 oz black grapes
caster sugar
whipped cream

Preparation time: 20 minutes, plus setting time

Dissolve three-quarters of one of the jelly tablets in 300 ml/½ pint boiling water. Stir in the lemon juice and make up to 400 ml/scant ¾ pint with cold water. Leave in a cold place until on the point of setting. Fold in the grapes and spoon into a lightly greased or well rinsed-out 1.2 litre/2 pint mould. Chill until set. Meanwhile, dissolve the remaining jelly tablet in 200 ml/8 fl oz boiling water and leave in a cold place until on the point of setting.

Heat most of the milk in a small pan; mix the remainder with the custard powder and sugar. Pour on the hot milk, return to the pan and bring to the boil, stirring. Simmer for 1 minute or until thickened. Cover tightly and leave to cool.

Beat the soured cream into the custard. Whisk the jelly lightly, then fold evenly through the custard mixture. Pour quickly over the set jelly in the mould and leave in the refrigerator overnight to set.

Lightly whisk the egg white. Dip the black grapes first into the egg white and then roll in caster sugar to give a frosted effect. Leave to set. Turn out the bavarois on to a serving plate. Decorate around the top or sides with cream and frosted grapes.

Getting organized

Brisket takes a long time to cook, but once in the oven it requires very little attention. Serve with buttered peas and creamed potatoes. The starter may be partially prepared in advance (hard-boiling the eggs and making the mayonnaise sauce) and completed just before serving. The gâteau must be baked the day before, and is best assembled several hours beforehand.

Egg and tomato mayonnaise

Metric

lettuce leaves
6 large tomatoes, sliced
6 hard-boiled eggs
150 ml thick mayonnaise
1 × 15 ml spoon lemon
    juice
2–3 × 15 ml spoons cream
    or top of the milk
large pinch of curry
    powder or a few crops
    of anchovy essence
salt
freshly ground black
    pepper

To garnish:

1 × 50 g can anchovy
    fillets, drained
watercress

Imperial

lettuce leaves
6 large tomatoes, sliced
6 hard-boiled eggs
¼ pint thick mayonnaise
1 tablespoon lemon
    juice
2–3 tablespoons cream or
    top of the milk
large pinch of curry
    powder or a few drops
    of anchovy essence
salt
freshly ground black
    pepper

To garnish:

1 × 2 oz can anchovy
    fillets, drained
watercress

Preparation time: about 15 minutes

Arrange several lettuce leaves on six small plates. Make a circle of tomato on each. Cut the tip off each egg so it will balance and stand it carefully in the centre of the tomato circle, or cut each egg in half and lay the halves on the tomatoes.

Beat the mayonnaise, lemon juice and sufficient cream together to give a smooth coating consistency, then add curry powder or anchovy essence and salt and pepper to taste. Spoon over the eggs to coat completely. Garnish with anchovy fillets and sprigs of watercress. Serve with toast or hot crispy bread and butter.

Pot roast brisket of beef

Metric	Imperial
1 × 1½–1¾ kg lean brisket of beef, boned and rolled	1 × 3½–4 lb lean brisket of beef, boned and rolled
150 ml white wine or cider	¼ pint white wine or cider
1 sprig each of fresh thyme and fresh rosemary, or 1 bouquet garni	1 sprig each of fresh thyme and fresh rosemary, or 1 bouquet garni
2–3 bay leaves	2–3 bay leaves
8 cloves	8 cloves
3 × 15 ml spoons dripping or oil	3 tablespoons dripping or oil
12 small onions, peeled	12 small onions, peeled
12 medium carrots, peeled	12 medium carrots, peeled
2 turnips, peeled and quartered, or 1 small swede, peeled and roughly chopped	2 turnips, peeled and quartered, or 1 small swede, peeled and roughly chopped
300 ml beef stock	½ pint beef stock
salt	salt
freshly ground black pepper	freshly ground black pepper
2–3 × 5 ml spoons cornflour (optional)	2–3 teaspoons cornflour (optional)

Preparation time: about 15 minutes, plus 3–4 hours marinating time
Cooking time: about 4 hours
Oven: 160°C, 325°F, Gas Mark 3

Place the joint in a bowl and pour over the wine or cider and add the thyme, rosemary or bouquet garni, bay leaves and cloves. Leave for several hours to marinate, turning it over two or three times. Remove the meat, reserving the marinade, and pat dry with kitchen paper.

Heat the dripping or oil in a frying pan, add the joint and fry until well browned all over, including the ends. Transfer to a large deep casserole. Arrange the vegetables around the joint, then add the stock, reserved marinade and plenty of salt and pepper. Cover and cook in a preheated oven for about 4 hours or until tender. (A little extra stock may be added during cooking, but should not be necessary.)

Place the joint on a heated serving dish. Drain the vegetables and arrange around the meat. Keep warm. Strain the pan juices into a small pan, spooning off any excess fat. Add the cornflour dissolved in a little cold water, bring to the boil and simmer for 1–2 minutes. Adjust the seasoning and pour into a sauce-boat.

Pineapple gâteau

Metric	Imperial
3 eggs	3 eggs
100 g caster sugar	4 oz caster sugar
100 g self-raising flour	4 oz self-raising flour
1 × 425 g can pineapple rings	1 × 15 oz can pineapple rings
little sherry (optional)	little sherry (optional)
450 ml double cream	¾ pint double cream
50 g flaked almonds, toasted	2 oz flaked almonds, toasted
maraschino or glacé cherries, to decorate	maraschino or glacé cherries, to decorate

Preparation time: about 30 minutes, plus chilling time
Cooking time: 20–25 minutes
Oven: 190°C, 375°F, Gas Mark 5

Whisk the eggs and sugar together until very thick and the whisk leaves a trail when removed. Sift the flour twice and fold through the whisked mixture. Turn into a greased and lined 18 × 28 cm/7 × 11 inch shallow cake tin and level the top. Bake in a preheated oven for 20–25 minutes or until well risen, firm and golden. Turn on to a wire rack and leave to cool.

Drain the pineapple, reserving the syrup. Set aside three rings, then chop the remainder. Cut the cake in half lengthwise and place one piece on a plate or board. Sprinkle with 2 × 15 ml spoons/2 tablespoons of the pineapple syrup mixed with a little sherry.

Whip the cream until stiff and mix about one quarter of it with the chopped pineapple. Spread over the cake on the plate. Place the second piece of cake on top and mask completely with most of the remaining cream. Cover the sides evenly with toasted almonds. Cut the reserved pineapple rings in half and arrange in a line along the length of the cake. Put the remaining cream into a piping bag fitted with a star nozzle and pipe lines between the pineapple rings to hold them in place, as well as around the top edge of the gâteau and down each corner. Complete the decoration with cherries and any remaining toasted almonds. Chill for at least 30 minutes before serving.

Getting organized

Soup is the ideal choice for a starter you can prepare ahead of time and store in the refrigerator. The topping and batter for the chicken can also be made the day before, ready for immediate use. Serve baked jacket potatoes and a tossed mixed salad with the main course. Caramelized oranges improve with keeping, as they mature in the syrup.

Cauliflower and mushroom soup

Metric	Imperial
50 g butter or margarine	2 oz butter or margarine
1 onion, peeled and chopped	1 onion, peeled and chopped
225 g mushrooms, chopped	8 oz mushrooms, chopped
1.2 litres chicken stock	2 pints chicken stock
1 small cauliflower, cut into florets	1 small cauliflower, cut into florets
1 × 15 ml spoon lemon juice	1 tablespoon lemon juice
salt	salt
freshly ground black pepper	freshly ground black pepper
150 ml double cream	¼ pint double cream
mint or parsley sprigs, to garnish	mint or parsley sprigs, to garnish

Preparation time: 15 minutes
Cooking time: 25–30 minutes

Melt the butter or margarine in a saucepan, add the onion and fry gently until soft. Add the mushrooms and continue cooking for 2–3 minutes. Stir in the stock, cauliflower, lemon juice and salt and pepper, and bring to the boil. Cover and simmer gently for 25–30 minutes until the cauliflower is very tender. Cool slightly, then sieve or liquidize the soup and return it to a clean pan. Adjust the seasoning and bring back to the boil. Stir in the cream, reheat without boiling and serve topped with mint or parsley.

Herb baked chicken with corn fritters

Metric
6 chicken breasts, boned
salt
freshly ground black
    pepper
25 g butter, softened
oil
8 × 15 ml spoons fresh
    breadcrumbs
1 × 15 ml spoon chopped
    fresh parsley
1½ × 5 ml spoons dried
    mixed herbs
40 g salted peanuts,
    chopped

Imperial
6 chicken breasts, boned
salt
freshly ground black
    pepper
1 oz butter, softened
oil
8 tablespoons fresh
    breadcrumbs
1 tablespoon chopped
    fresh parsley
1½ teaspoons dried mixed
    herbs
1½ oz salted peanuts,
    chopped

Corn fritters:
1 egg
3 × 15 ml spoons plain
    flour
4 × 15 ml spoons milk
1 × 15 ml spoon finely
    chopped onion
1 × 300 g can sweetcorn
    kernels, drained
oil for frying

Corn fritters:
1 egg
3 tablespoons plain
    flour
4 tablespoons milk
1 tablespoon finely
    chopped onion
1 × 11 oz can sweetcorn
    kernels, drained
oil for frying

Preparation time: 20 minutes
Cooking time: about 1 hour
Oven: 200°C, 400°F, Gas Mark 6

Season the chicken pieces with salt and pepper, then rub all over with the softened butter. Place in a roasting tin and pour over 2 × 15 ml spoons/2 tablespoons oil. Roast in a preheated oven for about 25 minutes, basting once with the fat in the tin.
Combine the breadcrumbs, parsley, mixed herbs and peanuts and season well with salt and pepper. Baste the chicken again and spoon the topping evenly all over it. Spoon a little of the fat in the tin over each portion and return to the oven. Roast for a further 20–25 minutes or until the chicken is tender and the topping golden brown and crispy.
Meanwhile make the fritters. Beat the egg and flour together until smooth, then stir in the milk followed by the onion, sweetcorn and salt and pepper to taste. Heat a little oil in a frying pan and fry spoonfuls of the fritter mixture until set and golden brown on both sides. Drain on kitchen paper and keep warm.
Drain the chicken and arrange on a heated serving dish, surrounded by the fritters.

Caramelized oranges

Metric
12 medium oranges
450 g granulated sugar
300 ml water
6 cloves

Imperial
12 medium oranges
1 lb granulated sugar
½ pint water
6 cloves

Preparation time: 30 minutes, plus chilling time.

Thinly pare the rind from 4 of the oranges, free of white pith. Cut this rind into very thin strips and place in a small pan. Cover with water, bring to the boil and simmer for 10 minutes or until tender. Drain, reserving 4 × 15 ml spoons/4 tablespoons liquid.
Cut the peel and pith away from all the oranges, reserving any juice. Cut each orange carefully into slices, discarding any pips, then either reassemble the oranges, secure with cocktail sticks and place in a bowl or simply lay the slices in the bowl. Sprinkle with the strips of orange rind.
To make the syrup, put the sugar and water in a heavy-based saucepan with the cloves and heat gently, stirring until the sugar has dissolved. Bring to the boil and boil hard, without stirring, until the syrup turns a caramel colour. Remove from the heat immediately and add the orange rind cooking liquid and any juice from the oranges. Heat gently if the syrup begins to set, then pour over the oranges. Cool, cover with cling film and refrigerate. Leave for at least 6 hours and preferably for 1–2 days before serving.
Discard the cloves and serve, with or without cream.

Getting organized

The day before par-cook the courgettes ready for grilling. Marinate the noisettes overnight. To serve creamed cauliflower and Parmentier potatoes divide a cauliflower into florets, peel and cube the potatoes. Make the hazelnut creams. One hour before the meal start cooking the noisettes of lamb. Cook the cauliflower until tender, drain and mash with a little cream, 2 egg yolks, salt and pepper, then place in a serving dish. Stand the dish in a roasting tin of water and keep warm in the oven. Parboil the cubed potatoes, drain and fry them in butter and oil until golden. Keep warm in the oven. Grill the courgettes and serve.

Courgettes au gratin

Metric	Imperial
12 medium or 6 large courgettes, trimmed	12 medium or 6 large courgettes, trimmed
1 medium onion, peeled and finely chopped	1 medium onion, peeled and finely chopped
50 g butter	2 oz butter
2 × 15 ml spoons oil	2 tablespoons oil
1 garlic clove, peeled and crushed	1 garlic clove, peeled and crushed
salt	salt
freshly ground black pepper	freshly ground black pepper
175 g Cheddar cheese, grated	6 oz Cheddar cheese, grated

Preparation time: 15 minutes
Cooking time: 25 minutes

Cut the courgettes in half lengthways and place in a large flameproof pan with the onion, butter, oil, garlic, salt and pepper. Cover and cook gently for 15 minutes.
Sprinkle with the grated cheese. (The courgettes can be prepared to this stage and chilled overnight.)
Put the courgettes under a hot grill until the cheese topping is bubbling and golden. Light out with a slotted spoon and serve.

Noisettes of lamb with ginger and honey sauce

Metric	Imperial
6 large noisettes of lamb	6 large noisettes of lamb
4 × 15 ml spoons ginger wine	4 tablespoons ginger wine
4 cloves	4 cloves
juice of 1 lemon	juice of 1 lemon
1 × 15 ml spoon soft brown sugar	1 tablespoon soft brown sugar
salt	salt
freshly ground black pepper	freshly ground black pepper
4–6 × 15 ml spoons clear honey	4–6 tablespoons clear honey
2 × 15 ml spoons coarsely chopped fresh mint	2 tablespoons coarsely chopped fresh mint

Preparation time: 15 minutes, plus marinating time
Cooking time: 40–50 minutes
Oven: 190°C, 375°F, Gas Mark 5

Put the noisettes into a shallow dish or container, then pierce each noisette several times with a skewer. Spoon over the ginger wine and add the cloves, lemon juice, brown sugar, and salt and pepper. Cover the dish with cling wrap and chill overnight.
Remove the noisettes from the marinade and put into a shallow ovenproof dish. Cook in a preheated oven for 10 minutes.
Heat the honey in a small pan with the marinade and spoon over the noisettes. Continue cooking for a further 30 to 35 minutes, until the noisettes are just tender. Sprinkle with chopped mint before serving.

Hazelnut creams

Metric	Imperial
450 ml double cream	¾ pint double cream
3 egg whites	3 egg whites
100 g caster sugar	4 oz caster sugar
100 g flaked hazelnuts	4 oz flaked hazelnuts
few whole hazelnuts	few whole hazelnuts
3 × 15 ml spoons coarsely grated plain chocolate	3 tablespoons coarsely grated plain chocolate

Preparation time: 20 minutes, plus chilling time

Whip the cream until it is thick. Beat the egg whites until they are stiff. Add the caster sugar to the egg whites and continue beating until they hold in stiff peaks. Fold the beaten egg whites lightly into the cream, together with the flaked hazelnuts. Spoon the mixture into six cocotte dishes and chill in the refrigerator overnight.
Decorate each nut cream with one or two whole hazelnuts and a sprinkling of coarsely grated chocolate just before serving.

Getting organized

A celebration dinner such as this one requires a lot of preparation amidst the usual chaos of a family Christmas, but careful planning ahead of time will help you through the day. The cocktails may be made the day before and refrigerated, as can the stuffing, giblet stock and brandy butter. Vegetables and bread sauce can be prepared and everything put ready to cook. This leaves only the turkey to be stuffed and put in the oven, the pudding to be put on to boil and vegetables to be cooked on the day, giving you plenty of time to be with the family. Remember to cool leftover turkey as quickly as possible and when cold to put it into the refrigerator.

St Nicholas cocktails

Metric	Imperial
1 large ogen melon	*1 large ogen melon*
4 large grapefruits	*4 large grapefruits*
100 g black grapes, halved and pipped	*4 oz black grapes, halved and pipped*
175 g green grapes, halved and pipped	*6 oz green grapes, halved and pipped*
175 g fresh dates, halved and stoned	*6 oz fresh dates, halved and stoned*
mint or parsley sprigs, to garnish	*mint or parsley sprigs, to garnish*

Preparation time: about 25 minutes

Halve the melon, remove the seeds and cut the flesh into balls or small cubes; put into a bowl. Cut the grapefruits in half, making a zig-zag pattern on the edges if possible, then carefully cut out all the flesh. Discard the membrane and seeds and add the pieces of flesh to the melon with any grapefruit juice. Add the grapes and dates to the bowl, mix well and spoon back into the grapefruit shells, with a little juice. Chill thoroughly, then garnish with mint or prasley.

Roast turkey with nut and raisin stuffing

Metric
1 × 4½–5½ kg oven-ready
  turkey
1 onion, peeled

Stuffing:
25 g butter
1 small onion, peeled and
  chopped
75 g fresh breadcrumbs
40 g salted peanuts,
  chopped
50 g seedless raisins,
  chopped
grated rind of 1 orange
2 × 15 ml spoons chopped
  fresh parsley
1 × 2.5 ml spoon dried
  thyme
salt
freshly ground black
  pepper
beaten egg, to bind

To garnish:
watercress
orange slices

Imperial
1 × 10–12 lb oven-ready
  turkey
1 onion, peeled

Stuffing:
1 oz butter
1 small onion, peeled and
  chopped
3 oz fresh breadcrumbs
1½ oz salted peanuts,
  chopped
2 oz seedless raisins,
  chopped
grated rind of 1 orange
2 tablespoons chopped
  fresh parsley
½ teaspoon dried
  thyme
salt
freshly ground black
  pepper
beaten egg, to bind

To garnish:
watercress
orange slices

Preparation time: 30 minutes
Cooking time: 3–3¼ hours
Oven: 180°C, 350°F, Gas Mark 4

If using a frozen bird make sure it is completely thawed out – allowing at least 24 hours at room temperature for this size of turkey. It is a good idea to calculate so that the bird is cooked 15–20 minutes before it is served; this allows time for it to set and makes carving easier, or it allows extra time if it is not quite cooked.

Remove the giblets from the turkey and put them in a saucepan with the onion. Cover with water, bring to the boil and simmer for 1 hour.
Meanwhile to make the stuffing, melt the butter in a frying pan, add the onion and fry gently until golden. Turn into a bowl and mix in the breadcrumbs, peanuts, raisins, orange rind, parsley, thyme, salt and pepper. Add sufficient beaten egg to bind the mixture. Wipe the bird inside and out with a clean cloth, then stuff the neck end with the stuffing. Secure the neck flap with a small skewer. Make any remaining stuffing into balls the size of a walnut. Place the turkey in a large roasting tin and rub all over with a little softened butter or margarine. Season lightly with salt and pepper. Roast in a preheated oven for 3–3¼ hours, basting from time to time and laying foil over the breast and legs when sufficiently browned. A skewer inserted into the deepest part of the turkey's thigh should show clear juices when it is cooked; if they are pink, return the bird to the oven for a further 15 minutes roasting, then test again.
For roast potatoes arrange peeled and parboiled potatoes around the bird 1½ hours before it is ready. Cook bacon rolls, chipolatas and any stuffing balls in a separate tin in the oven for about 30 minutes or under the grill.
Serve the turkey on a large platter with chipolatas and bacon rolls around it and garnished with watercress and orange slices. Serve with gravy made from the strained giblet stock and pan juices, bread sauce, roast potatoes, Brussels sprouts and buttered carrots.

Christmas pudding

Preparation time: 30–40 minutes
Cooking time: 7–8 hours, then 3–4 hours reboiling before serving

Metric

100 g sultanas
100 g currants
100 g seedless raisins, chopped
50 g chopped mixed peel
50 g glacé cherries, chopped
50 g blanched almonds, chopped
50 g ground almonds
100 g golden syrup
100 g fresh breadcrumbs
1 carrot, peeled and grated
100 g shredded suet
1 apple, peeled, cored and grated
1 × 1.25 ml spoon ground cinnamon
1 × 1.25 ml spoon mixed spice
100 g demerara or soft brown sugar
grated rind and juice of 1 lemon
little grated orange rind (optional)
2 eggs (sizes 1, 2)
3 × 15 ml spoons brandy
4–5 × 15 ml spoons brown ale
little lard for greasing basin

Imperial

4 oz sultanas
4 oz currants
4 oz seedless raisins, chopped
2 oz chopped mixed peel
2 oz glacé cherries, chopped
2 oz blanched almonds, chopped
2 oz ground almonds
4 oz golden syrup
4 oz fresh breadcrumbs
1 carrot, peeled and grated
4 oz shredded suet
1 apple, peeled, cored and grated
$\frac{1}{4}$ teaspoon ground cinnamon
$\frac{1}{4}$ teaspoon mixed spice
4 oz demerara or soft brown sugar
grated rind and juice of 1 lemon
little grated orange rind (optional)
2 eggs (sizes 1, 2)
3 tablespoons brandy
4–5 tablespoons brown ale
little lard for greasing basin

Put all the ingredients into a large bowl in the order they appear and mix very well together. Grease a 1.2 litre/2 pint pudding basin liberally with lard and spoon in the mixture. Cover the basin first with a double layer of well greased greaseproof paper and then with a pudding cloth or foil. Tie securely.

Place in a saucepan and add boiling water to come halfway up the side of the basin. Cover the pan and simmer gently for 7–8 hours, adding extra boiling water as necessary. Remove the pudding from the pan and allow to go cold.

Cover the basin with fresh greased greaseproof paper and a cloth or foil and store in a cool place until required. The pudding will keep for several months and should be made at least 2 months before Christmas to allow it time to mature. Boil as above for 3–4 hours before serving.

If silver coins are to be put into the pudding they should be soaked in boiling water, then wrapped in foil and inserted just before the pudding is taken to the table. To ignite the pudding, warm a little brandy in a saucepan or spoon, pour over the pudding and set alight. Serve with Brandy Butter and/or cream.

Brandy butter

Metric
100 g unsalted butter
225 g icing sugar, sifted, or
   175 g icing sugar and
   50 g light soft brown
   sugar
2–3 × 15 ml spoons
   brandy

Imperial
4 oz unsalted butter
8 oz icing sugar, sifted, or
   6 oz icing sugar and
   2 oz light soft brown
   sugar
2–3 tablespoons
   brandy

Preparation time: about 15 minutes

Beat the butter until soft, then gradually beat in the sugar alternately with the brandy. Place in a bowl, cover with cling film and chill until required.

Index